dr. samuel l. brown

wounds can heal
even if scars remain

healing emotional wounds
through the power of forgiveness

Wounds Can Heal, Even If Scars Remain
Copyright © 2023 by Samuel I. Brown

The Everyday Bible: New Century Version (Nashville, TN: Thomas Nelson, Inc., 2005)

The Holy Bible: English Standard Version (Wheaton, IL: Crossway Bibles, 2016)

The Holy Bible: Holman Christian Standard Version. (Nashville: Holman Bible Publishers, 2009)

The Holy Bible: King James Version, Electronic Edition of the 1900 Authorized Version. (Bellingham, WA: Logos Research Systems, Inc., 2009)

The New International Version (Grand Rapids, MI: Zondervan, 2011)

The New King James Version (Nashville: Thomas Nelson, 1982)

The Revised Standard Version (Oak Harbor, WA: Logos Research Systems, Inc., 1971)

Tyndale House Publishers, Holy Bible: New Living Translation (Carol Stream, IL: Tyndale House Publishers, 2015)

For information contact: www.shepublishingllc.com

Cover and Title Page Design by Michelle Phillips of CHELLD3 3D VISUALIZATION AND DESIGN

ISBN:
978-1-953163-84-4 (paperback)
978-1-953163-87-5 (hardback)

First Edition: December 2023

10 9 8 7 6 5 4 3 2 1

DEDICATION

This book, *Wounds Do Heal: Even If Scars Remain*, is a testament to the resilience of the human spirit, the strength of love, and more than anything, it is a tribute to your unwavering belief in me. Without you by my side, the pages of this book would remain empty, the words unspoken, and my dream unrealized.

To my wife, Danae, you have been my rock, and my inspiration during those times of uncertainty and doubt. Your encouragement and faith have been the fuel needed to face the depth of the wounds we carry, and the courage to acknowledge and confront them.

More than a rock, you have been my cheerleader and constant support. Your inspiring words have echoed in my ears, even in those late, sleepless nights, reliving the painful moments, nudging me to press forward, to heal, to grow, and to complete what was started. Your prayers and faith in me have been the beacon that has guided my hand as I penned each word, each sentence, and each chapter of our shared journey.

This book, then, is not only a dedication but a celebration of you, Danae. A celebration of your resilience, your belief, your unwavering love and the reason why we don't quit before we finish. Without you, *Wounds Do Heal: Even If Scars Remain* would merely be a dream, but with you, it is a reality. We are a team and I love you with all of me.

To my mother, who taught me to face my wounds with courage, and whose love and guidance have shaped me into the person I am today. You not only removed the cobwebs, but killed the spiders. You have shown me that even in the darkest moments, there is always hope as long as you trust in God, and that no wound is too deep to heal.

A special dedication to my father, who showed me what true strength and determination look like. Your memory will forever live on through the lessons you imparted and the love you gave us and I am forever grateful for the time we had together. You are my greatest hero, champion, and teacher, and most importantly, you were a man of faith and great courage. Your legacy will continue to live on through the many lives you've touched and the impact you've made. May your example continue to remind us that when we have God on our side, there is nothing that can stand against us. I will love you forever.

To my family and friends, thank you for your unwavering support and understanding throughout this journey. Your words of encouragement and love have been a constant source of inspiration and motivation.

And to all those who are struggling with their own wounds, whether physical or emotional, know that you are not alone. There is always hope for healing and growth, and it starts with acknowledging your wounds and having the courage to face them. You are stronger than you think and there is beauty in your scars.

Finally, I dedicate this book to all those who have been a part of my healing journey, whether knowingly or unknowingly. May these words serve as a beacon of hope and light for anyone in need of healing and may they inspire you to never give up on yourself. Remember, wounds do heal, even if scars remain. Don't ever quit before you finish your journey!

Samuel I. Brown

FOREWORD

Dr. Samuel I. Brown is a minister, educator, advocate, and my husband. As a survivor of childhood trauma himself, he provides a unique perspective on the healing process. His personal experiences and professional expertise make him a compassionate and understanding guide for those seeking to overcome emotional pain and build resilience. In addition, Dr. Brown also draws upon his years of experience as a minister and educator to provide spiritual insight and practical advice for readers on their journey toward healing. With his combination of personal experiences and professional knowledge, Dr. Brown offers a unique perspective on the topic of emotional healing.

This book can be beneficial for readers in several ways. Firstly, it provides a step-by-step guide for individuals to understand and overcome their emotional pain. It offers practical tools and techniques for managing difficult emotions and building resilience. Additionally, the book also provides valuable insight into the impact of past experiences on our present emotions and behaviors. This knowledge can help readers gain a better understanding of themselves and their past experiences, which can help them overcome emotional pain through forgiveness.

The central theme of this book is the transformative and healing power of forgiveness. It stands out from others in the same genre or topic area because it combines personal experiences, professional expertise, and spiritual insight to offer a well-rounded perspective on emotional healing. Dr. Brown's unique background as a survivor of childhood trauma allows him to connect with readers on a deeper level, and his experience as a pastor and formal educator provides relatable examples and advice. Additionally, this book sets an excellent foundation to be shared, whether in personal study or group study sessions.

This book addresses a wide range of emotional wounds, and it is interesting how it explores their roots from a unique perspective and equips us readers with practical solutions for healing through understanding, acceptance, and forgiveness. The book brings us face-to-face with our own feelings of guilt, anger, bitterness, and resentment head-on, and it is this confrontation that challenges us to do, think, and be better versions of ourselves.

I've personally had the experience of watching Dr. Brown overcome some traumatic experiences from his childhood. Seeing both the pain he experienced, and his growth expressed within the pages of this book and knowing how he has been able to apply the process of forgiving and letting go has been life-changing for me. I strongly believe that the experiences shared not only transformed his own life but will also help others heal through forgiveness.

This book is more than just a compilation of knowledge and advice; it carries a message of hope and healing for anyone who has gone through traumatic experiences. I have seen firsthand how his insights and guidance have transformed the lives of many individuals who were struggling with emotional wounds.

I found the chapter "We Are God's Masterpiece: Understanding Our Emotions" based on "I will praise You, for I am fearfully and wonderfully made. Marvelous are Your works, and that my soul knows very well." Psalm 139:14 (NKJV). Most Christians, at least internally, resist the idea that we were created to be God's masterpiece in a world fraught with evil, sin, despair, conflict, and pain. Then we find out that some of these issues are not just out there; they are inside of us as well. I wrote a short message for my husband based on this verse, but it was from a passage in Ephesians 2:10, "For we are God's masterpiece. He has created us anew in Christ Jesus, so we can do the good things he planned for us long ago" (NLT). We spend a lot of time condemning ourselves, not realizing how loved, redeemed, and valuable we are to God. This particular chapter resonated with me because it addresses a common struggle that many of us face: feeling unworthy and unlovable due to our past experiences or mistakes. Look back on your life. How much time have you spent analyzing, critiquing, and condemning yourself? Defining yourself? Dr. Brown's insights on how God sees us as His masterpiece despite our imperfections were truly eye-opening and comforting. This chapter addresses a deep truth that many of us struggle with. Dr. Brown's perspective on this topic was eye-opening and provided a refreshing and empowering viewpoint.

By: Danae S. Morris-Brown, MPA, MTRDV

CONTENTS

ACKNOWLEDGMENTS

I thank God for allowing me to write this book. Every person we encounter on our journey, whether they offer assistance or not, plays a vital role in our growth and transformation. I am profoundly thankful for both those who have supported me and those who have challenged me, as they've all contributed to shaping the remarkable person I am today.

Looking back on my past, I realize that every obstacle I faced, every hurt I experienced, and every moment of happiness I experienced have all led me to this central point. I am forever thankful for everything life has thrown my way, for it has given me the strength to grow, evolve, and become the best version of myself.

I thank my parents for the gift of life, for without them, I would not have been introduced to life. I would like to thank my friends and family for their support and encouragement throughout the years. I thank those who have shared their stories with me. Your strength has inspired me to continue writing, where I can offer comfort, understanding, and hope. To my wife, who stood by my side through the arduous process and countless sleepless nights, your unwavering belief in me and your enduring patience and nudges made the realization of this book possible. Your love and support have been my anchor, and I am forever grateful for your presence in my life.

And lastly, to you, dear reader, thank you for picking up this book and embarking on this journey with me. It is your curiosity and willingness to explore new worlds through words that keep the flame of storytelling alive. I hope the pages that follow offer you the same comfort, understanding, and hope that your stories have given me.

Finally, I am thankful that wounds can heal, even if the scars remain. I have come to recognize the healing power of forgiveness, and I want to share this knowledge with others. By forgiving, we are not condoning the hurtful actions of another, but we are taking a step toward our healing. We can finally make peace with the past and move forward with our lives.

My hope for this book is that it will help you find the courage and strength to forgive yourself and others so that you can move on and reclaim your beautiful life.

With deep gratitude,
Your Author,
Samuel I. Brown

WOUNDS CAN HEAL:
Even If Scars Remain

Are you struggling to move on from the emotional pain of your past? Have you ever wondered if it is possible to forgive and heal from the wounds of your experiences? In this book, *Wounds Can Heal: Even if Scars Remain*, I will share important strategies to assist you in finding a path to forgiveness and true healing.

Through inspiring stories, practical tips, and insights, I will guide you on your own journey toward healing the hurts, pain, and wounds that linger in your past. You will learn how to recognize and accept what has happened, how to release the hurtful emotions that keep you trapped in pain and anger, and how to open yourself to the possibility of genuine healing and forgiveness.

We will explore the power of forgiveness, including self-forgiveness, the significance of living in the present, and how to practice radical acceptance—even when it feels like nothing can ever make things right again. Through the experiences and stories of those who have walked a similar path, you will be inspired to acknowledge what has happened and ultimately gather the courage to forgive, enabling you to move forward in your life.

You may believe it is impossible to heal from emotional pain and past hurt, but with dedication, self-compassion, self-love, and the divine power that only God can provide, true healing is attainable. Allow this book to serve as your guide on your journey toward recovery, where you will discover the strength of forgiveness and unlock inner peace.

This book was written with the intention of helping you find peace after experiencing emotional pain and hurt in the past. It is my sincere hope that you can discover healing within its pages and be inspired by the stories of those who have trodden a similar path. May this book be a blessing to you as you navigate this challenging journey toward healing and inner peace. My prayer is that this book will lead you to find ways to forgive those who have hurt you, heal from the wounds of your past, and move forward in your life with renewed hope and strength, even if the scars remain.

UNDERSTANDING THE POWER *of* FORGIVENESS

"Bear with each other and forgive each other. If someone does wrong to you, forgive that person because the Lord forgave you." Colossians 3:13 (NCV)

Forgiveness is a complex and often misunderstood concept. In this chapter, we will discuss why forgiveness is important, its practical application in everyday life, and the different types of forgiveness. We will also touch on how forgiving is beneficial for our own mental health and well-being and how it can help us heal from emotional wounds.

She was mentally and emotionally imprisoned. Her heart filled with bitterness, anger, and resentment. It weighed her down like an anchor, dragging her deeper into the depths of despair. She felt like she was trapped in a prison of her own making, unable to escape or even see beyond her feelings of hurt and disappointment.

Abused and molested as a child, she was left with a deep sense of shame and regret, unable to forgive either of the perpetrators or herself. She went through her younger years, considered by others to be an outcast. This caused her to become more reclusive, which ultimately affected her self-esteem. She built an impenetrable wall of pain and despair, believing that she deserved to suffer.

She tried to find solace in the everyday routines of life and even tried to just forget about the experiences, but the pain and suffering she felt from her inability to forgive were always there to remind her and kept her locked into a mental battlefield. The more she tried to break away from the chains of unforgiveness, the closer it brought her back. She felt this cycle of hurt, pain, and anguish was never ending. No matter what advice or suggestions were given, she could not shake the pain of her past trauma and the emotional hurt that she suffered. How would it be possible for a person to appear normal but feel so broken inside? Even worse, how could a person with a strong connection to church be so wounded?

Although she served in the church and others looked up to her, she was so lost in her thoughts and emotions that she could not find a way to break free from her mental imprisonment. Through a series of unfortunate events, all three perpetrators died, leaving her without closure. How can you forgive someone without a genuine apology? How can you move forward without closure? She wanted to feel free, but no matter how hard she tried, it felt impossible—until one day when she finally realized to break free from her unforgiveness, she had to truly forgive.

Forgiveness is an act of grace to be extended to others even when we are hurt or aggrieved[1]. Colossians 3:13 (NCV) states, "Bear with each other, and forgive each other. If someone does wrong to you, forgive that person because the Lord forgave you." This verse calls us to forgive others and reflect God's love in our lives. This is important as it is a reminder that forgiveness is not merely a feeling but an action. As you are reading this, you are probably recalling a significant time in your life and picturing that person who hurt you, abused you, mishandled you, mismanaged your emotions, embarrassed you, and made you feel less than a person. Maybe you are picturing them and feeling the hurt, pain, and anger that has been deep-rooted in your heart for years. You may remember vividly how it felt when they hurt you and how much that person changed your life. You can choose to allow the hurt and anger to linger in your heart, or you can choose to forgive.

Although the word "forgiveness" is used frequently, we plan to delve deeper to discuss what is called "true forgiveness." While we may mention forgiveness, it is important to note that that emphasis will be intentionally placed on true forgiveness. Forgiveness and true forgiveness, while related, differ in their depth and implications. Forgiveness is often viewed as releasing

---

[1] *Merriam-Webster*.com Dictionary, s.v. "forgiveness," accessed October 5, 2015, https://www.*Merriam-Webster*.com/dictionary/forgiveness.

resentment or anger toward someone who has caused harm, an action taken for personal peace and moving forward. On the other hand, true forgiveness goes beyond that. It entails not only letting go of negative emotions but also gaining a complete understanding of the other person's perspective, which leads to empathy and compassion. This transformation allows for a perspective free of bitterness or resentment. Although the distinction between forgiveness and true forgiveness is subtle, it is important to differentiate between a surface-level release and a profound internal change.

Forgiveness is a decision and a process[2]. Why is it a process? The process of moving from a state of hurt and pain to a state of peace and healing requires time. At the same time, forgiveness should not be taken lightly. The Bible speaks of consequences for offenses done against another person or God. Galatians 6:7 (KJV) says, "Be not deceived; God is not mocked: for whatsoever a man soweth, that shall he also reap."

This verse speaks to the fundamental principle and law of cause and effect[3], also known to circles outside of Christianity as karma, states that every action has a consequence. In Galatians 6:7, the Apostle Paul is warning

---

[2] Enright, Robert. *Forgiveness Is a Choice: A Step-by-Step Process for Resolving Anger and Restoring Hope.* Ebook. American Psychological Association, 2001.

[3] Lewis, David. "Causation." *The Journal of Philosophy* 70, no. 17 (1973): 556–67. https://doi.org/10.2307/2025310.

the Galatians against the deception of thinking that they can mock God and avoid the consequences of their actions. He is reminding them that they will reap what they sow, whether it be good or bad.

This idea is not unique to Christianity. It is a universal principle that is found in many religions and philosophical traditions. However, Paul is specifically addressing the Galatians in their Christian context, reminding them that their actions have eternal consequences. This verse emphasizes the importance of taking responsibility for one's actions and living a life that is aligned with God's will.

The concept of sowing and reaping can be applied to various areas of life. It reminds us that the choices we make today will affect our future. It emphasizes the importance of living with intention and purpose and making choices that align with our values and beliefs. It also reminds us that we cannot escape the consequences of our actions and that we must take responsibility for the impact that our choices have on ourselves and others.

Ultimately, the Bible teaches us to forgive others just as we have been forgiven by God. This is a difficult task and requires us to put aside our pride and prejudice to extend grace and mercy to those who have hurt us. With the help of God's spirit, we can learn to embrace forgiveness as a way of life and show love to those around us, even in difficult times.

God's infinite and unconditional love for each of us is the ultimate example of forgiveness. It reminds us that if God can forgive our sins, then we too can forgive one another. We are called to be vessels of mercy, grace, and love. We are called to love others even when it is hard and show mercy to those who have hurt us so that we can be an example of the restoration power of God's forgiveness.

Forgiveness is a powerful tool we can use to nurture our emotional well-being. It is an act of understanding, releasing, and moving forward. Forgiveness encompasses both the spiritual and the human side of man. From a Christian perspective, it means letting go of anger and resentment while offering grace and mercy. From a perspective not bound by religious beliefs, it is viewed as the act of releasing any stored resentments, letting go of grudges and accepting the wrongs of the past so that you can move on in peace.

No matter your religious or spiritual beliefs, forgiveness is an essential part of healing from past traumas[4]. If used effectively, it can allow the needed release from negative patterns and habits that have built up over time so that we can ultimately experience peace in our lives[5]. What's more, forgiveness helps us to break unhealthy attachments to people who have hurt us and replace them

---

[4] Reed, Gloria J. "Forgiveness as a Path to Healing and Reconciliation." *Journal of Psychology and Christianity*, 33, no. 1 (2014): 59-67.
[5] Luskin, Frederic. *Forgive for Good: A Proven Prescription for Health and Happiness*. Harper Collins, 2010.

with feelings of empathy and compassion instead[6]. Ultimately, embracing forgiveness is key to our personal growth and finding true healing along the way.

Forgiveness is an often overlooked and underestimated avenue of healing, whether physical or emotional. The willingness to forgive, whether to ourselves or to those who have hurt or aggrieved us, can be an incredibly powerful force of healing. Forgiveness is not easy nor a one-time act, but a journey that requires courage, patience, and commitment. Through the process of forgiving, individuals are often able to cope with situations more positively, let go of resentment, restore relationships, and gain greater peace of mind[7].

It is important to distinguish between forgiving and condoning a wrong that has been done. To forgive does not diminish responsibility for the offense, and it does not mean forgetting the experience of the wrong. Forgiveness is instead a process of understanding the humanity of the person who hurt you and of recognizing our own capacity for love, compassion, and mercy. It is about making a conscious decision to focus on something other than the wrong that has been done, to take the power away from an

---

[6] Karen, Robert, PhD. *The Forgiving Self: The Road from Resentment to Connection*. New York, United States of America: Anchor Books, 2011.

[7] Reed, Gloria J. "Forgiveness as a Path to Healing and Reconciliation." *Journal of Psychology and Christianity*, 33, no. 1 (2014): 59-67.

experience that has caused us pain. Emotional healing takes place as we learn to let go of resentment and bitterness in favor of understanding and compassion.

Condoning is often understood as an acceptance of a wrong that has been committed, without any judgment or change in behavior to rectify the wrongdoing[8]. It can be seen as a way of overlooking a mistake and allowing it to go unacknowledged, with no effort made toward healing or addressing the issue. It avoids any confrontation to address the issue head-on.

In contrast, forgiving is a much more conscious effort. It can involve both understanding and accepting the wrong that has been done, but it also involves actively working toward forgiveness and reconciliation. This can even include changing behavior in order to move past the hurtful act, which requires confrontation, if necessary. The focus of forgiveness is not just on the perpetrator, but also on those who have been hurt—both in terms of making an effort to heal the wounds and to restore balance in the relationship.

Another difference between condoning and forgiving is the level of understanding required for each. Condoning requires no understanding of the situation, as it is simply allowing something to continue without judgment. Forgiving requires a deep level of understanding, empathy,

---

[8] Pettigrove, Glen. "Unapologetic Forgiveness." *American Philosophical Quarterly* 41, no. 3 (2004): 187–204. http://www.jstor.org/stable/20010156.

and compassion in order to move forward from an event or hurtful situation.

Condoning can be seen as a more superficial way of dealing with and addressing issues, while forgiving takes time, effort, and understanding to truly move forward from an event. Forgiving requires a person to look beyond what has happened and find the strength to move on. It is an emotional process that can take time, but it ultimately allows for healing of the mind, body, and soul.

Forgiveness is not easy, but it is possible with faith in God and the strength He provides. When we forgive someone for what they have done, we choose to take the higher road—even if those actions hurt us or someone else. We can find healing and peace in knowing that, even if we can't excuse the wrong that has been done, God still loves and cares for those involved. We may never completely forget what has happened, but we can make a conscious effort to let go of pain, resentment, and unforgiveness.

When it comes to addressing someone's behavior, God constantly reminds us to love our neighbor as ourselves and extend grace even when it is hard to do. We must remember that it is our job to help our brothers and sisters learn from their mistakes and grow in wisdom, not simply forgive them for their offenses without holding them accountable. Why is accountability so important?

Accountability teaches us to take responsibility for our actions and learn from them so we can make wiser decisions in the future. Furthermore, accountability provides us with an opportunity to extend God's grace and love to others. We are called to forgive sins, not condone them—it is important that we show compassion rather than simply excusing behavior. By doing this, we empower others to make better decisions and learn from their mistakes in an environment that reflects a balance between showing mercy and holding someone accountable for their actions. When we extend grace to one another, it is a reflection of God's unconditional love for us—we can be forgiven even when we do not deserve it.

We have the fundamental responsibility to reflect the same mercy, grace, and love that God has shown us. It is important to remain impartial and firm in our convictions while remaining both fair and compassionate toward others. Even in the most difficult circumstances, we must remember the example that was provided for us. Not only was the example and blueprint provided for us, we were also given both capacity and power to complete the process. We are called to give second chances and help those who have gone astray find their way back to the path of righteousness. When it comes to dealing with our own offenses, we must keep in mind that God's love for us goes beyond our behavior; He loves us unconditionally and extends grace to us no matter how many times we stray. We can facilitate restoration and reconciliation in our relationships with those around us through the power of forgiveness. Ultimately, it is up to us to make sure that God's love and mercy reign supreme in all our interactions with others. There must be a healthy balance between showing compassion and holding someone accountable for their actions.

Forgiving someone can be one of the most difficult tasks we face in life. It goes against our natural instincts to let go of the pain and hurt caused by others. If we were to take a deeper look at the instinctual reflex or response when there is pain or emotional hurt, we would find that it is rooted in fear and not love. Love is unconditional, while fear judges and seeks revenge. Fear is what creates separation and pain. Fear is born from an experience or memory. We store memories of events both psychologically and physically. We may even replay these memories over and over in our minds, leading us to react with fear when something similar occurs again. Forgiveness is the way to break free from this cycle of fear and pain. It's not easy, but it can be done. If our intentions are pure, we can be confident in knowing that God will provide the strength we need to make decisions that are based on love and mercy. Through forgiveness, we open ourselves up to a greater understanding of God's love and grace. Psalm 86:15 (NIV) reads, "But you, Lord, are a compassionate and gracious God, slow to anger, abounding in love and faithfulness" which reminds us of God's unconditional love and mercy.

Forgiveness is an act of courage that can help us rebuild broken relationships, heal deep wounds, and provide a sense of closure that could open the door for peace. Together with God's grace, forgiveness helps us to live intentionally. By forgiving, we let go of resentments and grudges so that our lives can be focused on more meaningful pursuits. We make space for healing and growth, enabling us to learn from our mistakes and become more compassionate. We don't have to stay bound by negative emotions; instead, we can live our lives more purposefully and intentionally with a deep understanding of the power of grace and mercy in our lives.

When we understand the power of grace and mercy, we can live a life that is centered around gratitude. We become more aware of our blessings and recognize how good God is to us. Our perspective changes from one of negativity and sadness to one of hopefulness. Moreover, living a life of gratitude helps us to put things into perspective and focus on the good in our lives. We are reminded that all our mistakes and failures are not the end, but only a step on a journey toward growth. Living with gratitude helps us to be more open to others, forgiving them and loving them in a way that honors both our relationship with God and the person we are striving to be.

Forgiveness is about letting go of our hurt, anger, and pain toward someone who has hurt us; this shows our faith in God's power of love and mercy. Condoning, on the other hand, implies approval for a wrong that has been done, and this goes against our faith. With forgiveness comes peace and a sense of freedom that can only be found in the power of God's love. Letting go of our hurt and anger shows a strength of character that can only come with faith in God.

Forgiveness is a reflection of our faith in God's power to restore and renew broken relationships. Forgiving others helps to reshape and strengthen our faith in several ways.

Forgiveness demonstrates a strength of character as well as an acceptance of our pasts that, in turn, can help us to move forward with a healthier mindset. It creates a space of understanding and compassion that encourages us to move on without bitterness or resentment. It also allows us to be at peace with the past and to understand that we are not responsible for other people's mistakes. At the same time, it creates an opportunity to forgive ourselves and our own mistakes. This creates a spiritual space where there is room for growth, understanding, and healing.

The more we put it into practice on a regular basis, the more we build our faith in the process of redemption, and we can transform and heal all our relationships. Our faith is strengthened when we practice forgiveness, understanding that it has a powerful impact on our lives. We become more aware of how much strength and healing lies within us, and this awareness helps to renew our faith in ourselves and others. Forgiveness isn't always easy, but it is always worth it. Through forgiveness we can experience true freedom—freedom from bitterness and anger that weigh us down and keep us from living in peace.

Forgiveness is a virtue that must be cultivated and practiced daily for it to become part of who we are. We must remember that God does not condone wrong behavior. There are boundaries and expectations for what is acceptable in his presence, but He does offer us forgiveness when we seek it. In other words, He does not condone our sins, but He will forgive them when we repent. This is both the example and expectation that was set for us—to forgive others. But because of our human condition, this goes much further, even when we do not feel like it.

To strengthen our faith in God, understand His love and grace, and build strong relationships, it is essential to comprehend the power of forgiveness and actively choose to forgive. This is how we can be a reflection of God's unconditional love for us. Forgiveness gives us the opportunity to show mercy, understanding, and compassion to those around us even when it seems that we are unable to do it. It is only when we choose to forgive that we can experience the emotional freedom, true inner peace, and joy that comes with understanding the depth of God's love for us. Ultimately, forgiveness is an important part of our faith journey, and it is only when we make the commitment to forgive that we can experience restoration and renewal in our lives.

Reflection Questions

1. How have my past experiences with forgiveness influenced my current relationships and emotional well-being?

2. What are some barriers that I face when it comes to forgiveness? How can I work to overcome these barriers?

3. How has forgiveness impacted my spiritual or religious beliefs?

4. How do I typically approach forgiveness in relationships? Is there a more effective approach that I could try?

5. Have I experienced self-forgiveness? What can I do to cultivate a greater sense of self-compassion and forgiveness?

6. How has forgiveness impacted my personal growth and emotional healing? What steps can I take to continue to cultivate forgiveness in my life?

THE COMPLEXITIES
of FORGIVENESS:
From History to Significance

"Judge not, and you will not be judged; condemn not, and you will not be condemned; forgive, and you will be forgiven" Luke 6:37 (ESV)

In this chapter, we will take a deeper look into the complexities of forgiveness, exploring how the power of forgiveness has evolved and how it can be applied to our lives today. We will also look at some of the beliefs, practices, and rituals that various religious, spiritual, and philosophical communities have used to foster a greater understanding of the importance of forgiveness in their own lives.

The biblical complexity of forgiveness can be difficult to understand, but ultimately it reflects the power and magnitude of God's love. The Bible emphasizes that while we are all sinners capable of great harm and evil, God is willing to forgive any wrong done by us when we turn to him in repentance. Jesus taught his followers how to love others despite their sins and shortcomings, setting the tone for how Christians should forgive one another. The power of forgiveness is something that has been discussed throughout history. From the teachings of Jesus and the Bible to renowned philosophers and spiritual leaders, many have shared their wisdom on how vital it is to forgive those who have hurt us.

Forgiveness has been a topic of discussion in theology, psychology, and philosophy for centuries. Its earliest roots can be traced back to ancient religions such as Judaism and Christianity, which both have scriptures devoted to the concept of forgiving others and seeking forgiveness from God. This idea was further expanded upon by philosophers such as Immanuel Kant, who wrote extensively about the need for individuals to take responsibility for their actions and forgive those who have aggrieved, offended, or hurt them. In psychology, Carl Jung devoted much of his work to exploring the concept of forgiveness as a path toward inner peace.

Today, many different professionals have made contributions to the study of forgiveness and its role in our lives[9]. A large plethora of sources can be sought out to research the topic. Researchers have studied how forgiveness can help us heal from painful experiences, manage stress and conflict, improve our relationships, and even strengthen our physical health. Medical and other professional journal articles are widely available to explore the health benefits and other implications. Further research is being done to explore the positive effects that forgiveness can have on individuals, couples, families, and communities.

It is clear that the act of forgiving oneself or others is a powerful one and that it has been part of our lives since the dawn of time. By exploring its history and origin, we can gain a better understanding of how it can be used to benefit ourselves and those around us.

Forgiveness is an act of mercy and grace, a gift to humanity that transcends time. It has its origin in spiritual and religious traditions around the world. In Christianity, it is a cornerstone of the faith and an intrinsic part of Jesus's teachings. It is also found in other major religions such as Judaism, Islam, and Buddhism.

Forgiveness has been around since ancient times, with some of its earliest roots found in the Old Testament. Ancient Greek philosophers such as Plato and Aristotle wrote about the importance of forgiveness in moral and ethical contexts. The great philosophers Socrates, Plato, and

---

[9] Enright, Robert D., and Joanna North. 1998. *Exploring Forgiveness*. Univ of Wisconsin Press.

Aristotle all believed that for one to be virtuous, one must learn how to forgive others[10].

Forgiveness is a complex process, and it takes time to develop. It involves understanding the harm done and making an effort to reconcile with those who have harmed us. It can be a difficult journey, but it has the potential to lead to harmony and peace in our lives. We should always keep in mind that forgiveness is within our capability and it's never too late to seek redemption for ourselves or forgive someone who has harmed us. This is not a transactional exchange but, rather, an invitation to live a life of compassion and forgiveness.

God's mercy and grace, which are both the bedrock and foundation of forgiveness, are presented in the Scriptures and teach what forgiveness is as well as prescribed recommendations within any given scenario. Jesus taught us to forgive "seventy times seven" (Matthew 18:22 KJV). He emphasized this by forgiving those who had persecuted him even as he was dying on the cross. This powerful example continues to inspire us and encourages us to show forgiveness in our own lives.

Forgiveness is not merely a concept but an essential ingredient for personal growth and spiritual development. It's a challenging act, but its impact is boundless.

---

[10] Griswold, Charles L. *Forgiveness: A Philosophical Exploration*. New York, United States of America: Cambridge University Press, 2007.

In the Bible, Jesus teaches us about the virtue of forgiveness when he advises Peter to forgive others an infinite number of times.

Forgiveness is a necessary component of a just and equitable society[11]. It is an act of mercy and compassion, which seeks to address harm and injustice in a way that is both restorative and transformative. The call to forgive seventy-seven times is a reminder that forgiveness is not a one-time event, but an ongoing process that requires constant attention and effort.

Moreover, this verse also speaks to the idea of infinite compassion, which is another central concept in philosophy and religion. Infinite compassion refers to the idea that love and compassion are boundless and infinite and that they have the power to transform even the most difficult and challenging situations. Jesus's response to Peter's question is a reminder of the infinite compassion that God has for us and the infinite compassion that we are called to have for others.

Forgiveness is a powerful force that is evident throughout the Bible. From Joseph forgiving his brothers for selling him into slavery to Jesus's parable of the unmerciful servant, the act of forgiving has been consistently preached and practiced. As we learn from the parable of the prodigal son, we should welcome back those who have harmed us with open arms, just as a loving father would do for his

---

[11] Bash, Anthony. "Forgiveness and Christian Ethics." Philosophical Papers. Accessed October 8, 2015. https://philpapers.org/rec/BASFAC.

beloved child. It may not be easy, but forgiveness is a necessary step toward healing and moving forward.

God's grace is further demonstrated when we consider the parable of the unmerciful servant (Matthew 18:21–35 KJV). In this story, Jesus teaches us that if we have been forgiven much by God, then we must also show mercy to those who sin against us. This parable reminds us that God's compassion and mercy extend to all people, no matter what they have done.

When we reflect on these stories and others, the central message of forgiveness across scripture reminds us of the importance of extending grace in our own lives. When we forgive those who have aggrieved, offended, or hurt us, it helps to break the chains of resentment, bitterness, and hurt that can weigh us down. It helps to heal our relationships with others and brings us closer to God. The power of forgiveness is a profound reminder of God's unconditional love for us, and it can help set us free from the pain and suffering caused by unforgiveness. Forgiveness, compassion, and mercy are all part of God's plan to bring us closer to Him so that we can experience the fullness of life He has for us. Therefore, it is essential to remember that forgiveness does not only heal the one being forgiven, but also the one doing the forgiving. Don't hesitate to forgive others. By extending mercy and grace, you are participating in God's plan to unite us with Him. Although it might be difficult, forgiveness is a potent weapon that can bring tranquility into our lives. These stories demonstrate how God desires us to be forgiving, compassionate, and merciful.

Forgiveness is one of the most profound concepts, and it has its roots in both spirituality and psychology[12]. It takes courage and strength to let go of the resentment, anger, and pain caused by someone's actions. However, studies have proven that the ability to forgive is directly related to our own physical and emotional health[13]. When we forgive, we free ourselves from the burden of negative emotions and open ourselves to greater happiness, better relationships, and a more fulfilling life. Forgiveness is not an easy feat, but with practice and patience, it can transform us and those around us. So, let us embrace this concept of forgiveness and let go of the pain, resentments, and grudges.

Despite its long history, forgiveness is still a misunderstood concept today. Many people struggle with it and see it as an impossible task or something that should only be done if the other person deserves it. As previously stated, forgiveness isn't indicative of weakness. It is about recognizing the hurt and pain caused by someone's words or actions and forgiving them from a place of understanding and compassion.

Forgiveness is not only something we give to others; it is also something that we can give ourselves. Forgiving

---

[12] Fiske, Susan T., Daniel T. Gilbert, and Gardner Lindzey. 2010. *Handbook of Social Psychology, Volume 2*. John Wiley & Sons.
[13] Toussaint, Loren L., E. L. J. Worthington, and David R. Williams. *Forgiveness and health*. Springer Netherlands, 2015.

yourself for past mistakes or bad decisions is essential to move forward and become the best version of yourself. Why is it necessary to forgive yourself before forgiving someone else? Because if we are not able to forgive ourselves, it is harder to extend forgiveness and grace to others. No matter how hard it may be, extending forgiveness is an essential part of the human experience. It can be liberating and transformative. So don't forget that forgiving doesn't just heal the other person—it heals us too. How is this even possible? By allowing ourselves to be vulnerable, to recognize that we are never perfect and that our mistakes are part of the learning process. The fear of being vulnerable with an offender or the person who caused hurt or harm can be paralyzing. In cases of extreme trauma, healing can take time, and professional counseling may be needed[14]. It is important to begin the healing process by forgiving, even if we still feel hurt inside.

Forgiveness is a reflection of strength, not weakness. It takes a brave person to take the first step toward forgiveness, and this can lead to great healing, both mentally and physically. In times of difficulty, it is important to remember that forgiveness has the power to heal and transform our lives. Even in the darkest of times, forgiveness is a gift that you can give both yourself and others. It's never

---

[14] Hickman, Carolyn. *Forgiving When You Can't Forget: Releasing Fear and Trauma from Your Past So You Can Have Freedom in Your Future*, 2021.

too late to start the journey toward peace and healing, so have courage and take that first step by forgiving.

Forgiveness is a profound act that can transform relationships, heal the wounds of the past, and help us to move forward on our paths toward peace and understanding.

True forgiveness is a state of emotional and psychological freedom from the hurt, anger, resentment, and bitterness that can accompany being aggrieved, offended, or hurt[15]. It involves compassion for oneself and for the one who caused harm. It goes beyond simply forgetting or disregarding what has happened; true forgiveness requires a conscious effort to understand the situation from all perspectives without placing blame or judgment. True forgiveness doesn't necessarily mean that you agree with the past or have to forget it, but rather that you accept what happened and choose to move forward without bitterness or negative feelings. When done effectively, true forgiveness can lead to a greater sense of inner peace and improved relationships with others. It is an important part of living a healthy and balanced life. Moreover, it is a powerful expression of faith in God's sovereignty and trust that He has a plan for our lives despite the wrongs we have faced.

True forgiveness can bring healing to the depths of our souls and redemption from the pain caused by past hurts. It is a conduit of love that can bring transformation and growth. As we learn to forgive those who have aggrieved,

---

[15] Smedes, Lewis B. *The Art of Forgiving: When You Need to Forgive and Don't Know How*. New York: Ballantine Books, 1996.

offended, or hurt us, we begin to understand God's love for us in a deeper way. We recognize our own imperfections and come to acknowledge how much He loves us despite them. We can choose true forgiveness to free ourselves from the chains of pain, hurt, and bitterness that can prevent us from living a full and meaningful life.

True forgiveness is more than just saying the words "I forgive you." It involves releasing any resentment or anger toward the person who hurt us and allowing God's grace to cover our hearts. True forgiveness means letting go of bitterness, embracing mercy and compassion for those who hurt us, and praying for their restoration. True forgiveness does not mean justifying the wrong that was done, or forgetting what happened—it means accepting God's power to heal our brokenness and extend grace to us and those who hurt us. When we practice true forgiveness, it not only brings healing to ourselves but also to those around us.

Forgiveness can be a difficult concept to understand, especially when it comes to forgiving yourself or others. Self-forgiveness is the process of accepting and understanding your mistakes and moving forward from them in order to heal. It involves acknowledging the harm that has been done, recognizing the impact it had on you, learning from your mistakes so it does not happen again, and forgiving yourself for the mistakes that you have made. Similarly, forgiving others requires understanding and empathizing with their mistakes or offense, allowing yourself to let go of any resentment toward them, and granting a degree of mercy for what has happened. Both self-forgiveness and forgiveness of others can be incredibly difficult to do, but they are also essential in order to be healthy and successful. Ultimately, forgiveness is a journey that takes time and effort but is worth it if you want to enjoy life and have meaningful relationships with yourself and others.

By learning how to forgive, we can open up an entirely new world of possibilities. We become capable of understanding our own mistakes as well as the mistakes of others, and we become empowered to recognize both our own and other people's strengths. We also become able to accept the imperfections in all of us without judgment or resentment, allowing us to move forward in life with a newfound sense of peace and understanding. The ability to forgive is essential for living a healthy and fulfilling life and can open up a world of untapped potential for anyone who learns to do it.

At the end of the day, forgiveness is something that must be learned and practiced in order to reap its benefits. It takes effort, courage, and patience, but it is possible with dedication. Through forgiving ourselves and others we can unlock our fullest potential, find peace in our lives, and have meaningful relationships with ourselves and others. It is an invaluable and extraordinary gift and skill that has been given that everyone should strive to learn and practice in order to live the healthiest, most fulfilling life possible.

Forgiveness offers numerous spiritual and psychological benefits. Studies have shown that with forgiveness comes an increased sense of personal well-being, improved mental health, and reduced stress levels. Practicing forgiveness can help to break the patterns of negative thinking, as well as allow us to address difficult emotions in a healthier way. On a spiritual level, it can be seen as a way to let go of the past, releasing us from the chains of resentment and bitterness that can keep us trapped in cycles of pain. Forgiveness is not only a gift we give others—it is a gift we give ourselves. By allowing ourselves to let go, we can move toward a place of inner peace and joy, ultimately enriching our lives in the long term. Moreover, practicing self-love can enable us to show understanding and kindness toward ourselves and others.

Giving forgiveness is a valuable gift that we can offer ourselves and those around us. It has far-reaching spiritual and psychological benefits, which can have a profound impact on our lives. On a spiritual level, forgiveness is a demonstration of love—it is in recognizing that each person has their own struggles and mistakes to deal with and offering understanding and compassion instead of anger or judgment.

On a psychological level, forgiveness can be seen as an act of self-care. It involves letting go of resentment and pain so that we can move forward in our lives without being weighed down by the past. By releasing ourselves from grudges and negative emotions, we open up to a more positive state of being which impacts our self-concept.

At the end of the day, it is essential to remember that forgiveness takes time and effort. It requires patience and dedication in order to reap its full benefits, but it is worth the effort. As we learn to forgive ourselves and others, we open up an entirely new world of understanding. With it, we can truly become the healthiest and most successful versions of ourselves.

Forgiveness also brings peace of mind and emotional healing. By forgiving those who have hurt us, we can free ourselves from the prison of anger, hurt, and resentment that can often accompany unresolved conflicts. This inner peace can provide an emotional foundation for growth, allowing us to become more resilient, better able to cope with life's challenges, and ultimately lead a happier and more fulfilling life.

Forgiveness is also an important part of our faith. In the Bible, Jesus taught us that we are called to forgive others as we have been forgiven by God. Forgiving those who hurt us can be difficult, but it is also an essential part of living out our faith and walking in a path of righteousness.

Forgiveness can help us to be kinder and wiser people. By forgiving ourselves for our mistakes and releasing others from any blame or judgment we may have placed on them, we can come to accept both ourselves and others with greater understanding and compassion. This can be a powerful act of grace, making us more understanding and forgiving in the future.

Forgiveness has the power to bring us spiritual growth, emotional healing, inner peace, and ultimately greater joy and contentment in our lives. We each have the free will to choose forgiveness—so we must be intentional in receiving and offering it to others. It is a challenging process that involves both emotional and cognitive factors. Deciding to forgive can depend on various factors, including the severity of the offense, the nature of the relationship, and personal beliefs and values. It is not a one-time event but rather a journey that entails time and effort to work through. It often involves experiencing a range of feelings, such as anger, hurt, and sadness and may require confronting and handling these emotions to be able to move forward toward forgiveness.

Forgiveness is not an easy task, but it can be one of the most transformative experiences one can go through. It takes strength, courage, and humility to extend forgiveness to those who have wronged us. However, the rewards of forgiveness are immeasurable. It is not about letting the wrongdoer off the hook, but about taking back control of our own lives and emotions. Forgiveness can heal pain that justice alone cannot reach. It opens the door to reconciliation and allows us to truly understand the perspectives of others.

While justice is vital to prevent future harm and ensure accountability, it cannot do everything. Forgiveness goes beyond the bounds of justice and looks to the deeper wounds within. It challenges us to be better versions of ourselves and to cultivate a more peaceful world. Ultimately, forgiveness is not just an act toward others, but an act of self-love and growth. It enables us to let go of the past and to embrace a better future.

Sometimes, legal or social justice measures may need to be implemented in conjunction with forgiveness. It is up to the individual who has been wronged to decide whether they are ready and willing to forgive.

Keep in mind that forgiveness is a personal decision and cannot be forced upon someone. While we can encourage and facilitate the process, it is ultimately up to the individual to choose the path toward forgiveness.

Forgiveness is a complex yet rewarding process that requires empathy, understanding, and emotional and cognitive work. Although it can be arduous, forgiveness is a powerful tool for achieving healing, reconciliation, and personal growth. So don't give up just yet. Learn to forgive and experience its maximum benefits in your life.

Reflection
Questions

1. How has my understanding of forgiveness been shaped by my cultural background and personal experiences?

2. What historical or cultural factors have influenced the way that forgiveness is viewed in my community or society?

3. How does my understanding of forgiveness compare to the historical and cultural origins of forgiveness discussed in the chapter?

4. What is the role of forgiveness in my personal and/or spiritual beliefs? How has this changed over time?

5. What can I learn from the history and origins of forgiveness to help me navigate the forgiveness process in my own life?

Uncovering Emotional Wounds:
What Are They?

"He heals the brokenhearted and

binds up their wounds." Psalm 147 (ESV)

In this chapter, we explore emotional wounds, their nature, and how they can be identified. It references Psalm 147:3, which states that God heals those who are brokenhearted and mends their wounds.

We all experience emotional pain at some point in our lives, and it can be hard to move beyond these wounds. Have you ever considered what are your emotional wounds? Have you thought about various triggers or how they may have been formed or how they manifest from time to time? If we take a deeper dive, we can identify and address them. We can also discover how forgiveness may help to uncover and heal these struggles.

What are emotional wounds? They're the deep-rooted feelings of hurt and pain that can be caused by a traumatic event such as abuse or neglect[16]. These experiences leave us feeling broken, helpless, and vulnerable. We often don't realize the impact these wounds have on our lives until much later—possibly after years of denial. In some cases, it can be more difficult to recover.

The causes of emotional wounds vary from person to person. It could be something that happened in your childhood, an unresolved issue with a family member or friend, or even a traumatic experience. It can be difficult to identify and address these wounds, but it is essential if you want to heal from them.

Emotional wounds can manifest in different ways, showing up as memories we may prefer to forget[17]. Feelings of sorrow and deep grief are among these—a pain that needs close attention, crying out for acknowledgment and care. Difficulty trusting others is also often connected to emotional wounds. We may be overwhelmed by waves of anger or resentment directed at the person who caused our hurt—yet hope for inner peace at the end of the day. A fear of letting anyone get too close to us or finding true intimacy feels almost like an act of self-preservation. There have also been instances where physical illnesses emerge as a direct

---

[16] Mickley, J. R., and K. Cowles. "Ameliorating the Tension: Use of Forgiveness for Healing." *Oncology Nursing Forum* 28, no. 1 (January 2001): 31–37.

[17] Reed, Gloria J. "Forgiveness as a Path to Healing and Reconciliation." *Journal of Psychology and Christianity*, 33, no. 1 (2014): 59-67.

result of deep emotional trauma we carry inside us. It holds true that until our hearts are seen and healed, our minds and bodies won't feel fully liberated either.

Other signs that you may have an unresolved emotional wound include depression, anxiety, anger, fear, avoidance of certain people or activities, and even physical symptoms like headaches. It's also important to pay attention to your emotions and reactions—if something triggers a strong reaction for no apparent reason, it could be a sign that there is an emotional wound that needs to be addressed. No matter the cause, it's important to recognize and address these wounds in order to move forward and heal.

Are you feeling overwhelmed and out of touch with yourself? Emotional wounds can linger, often manifesting without prompting as depression, anxiety, anger, fear, and even physical aches or pains. Taking special note of your reactions in moments of strength or triggers can be a sign that an inability to work through the situation is stuck beneath the surface. They can also be the result of unresolved issues from our past that have been left unaddressed.

But despite how deep and painful these wounds can be, there is hope in God. He promises us that he will bind up our broken hearts and heal our emotional wounds (Isaiah 61:1). He also promises that we can draw strength and courage from Him (Isaiah 41:10). We serve a God of restoration and healing. He specializes in performing the most impossible and extreme tasks and has promised to bind up our broken hearts and comfort us as we recover from these deep wounds. In other words, He will not only just fix what is broken. We can turn to Him in our darkest moments knowing that His grace will meet us there and carry us through whatever comes our way. He reminds us that "the LORD is close to the brokenhearted and saves those who are crushed in spirit" (Psalm 34:18 NIV).

His power enables us to not only survive but to thrive. We can begin the process of healing by opening up our wounds and allowing Him to fill them with His love, grace, and mercy. As we draw close to Him, He can fill us with courage, strength, and hope. We can trust that His will is best and that He has a plan to bring beauty from our pain.

No matter what wounds we are carrying today, let us remember that God is a healer. He wants to take the broken pieces of our lives and make them into something beautiful. He can transform our sorrows into joy and give us peace that surpasses all understanding. Let us allow Him to be the balm for our brokenness, trusting in His healing power and grace every step of the way. He is closer than we think, and He loves us more than we can imagine. He is our hope, and in Him we find true healing and restoration. We can rest assured that whatever wounds we may have in this life, God is able to make us whole again.

To start on the journey to healing our emotional wounds, we must be honest with ourselves. Also, by acknowledging our hurt, we can begin to understand why it has been so hard for us to heal and move forward. We need to recognize that these hurts are real and take hold of us in numerous ways. Furthermore, it's crucial for us to face the truth about what happened and how its aftermath has shaped our lives—this can entail facing some difficult moments since oftentimes we may feel inclined toward denying or burying these pains away from further hurt. On the other hand, allowing ourselves to truly feel these emotions and accept them can be an important part of our healing process. It's also important to be willing to reach out for help and support.

We all live with emotional wounds, some seemingly buried deep within us, in order to insulate ourselves from that painful truth. But by courageously exploring them, we can uncover the reasons behind why such traumas affect us so intensely. Through that knowledge, we gain power over our emotions, along with a path to liberation, opening us up to a brighter future full of hope rather than fear. We can escape what binds us and confront anything preventing transformation head-on, for letting go means making room for growth and providing an opportunity to fully heal those buried wounds from long ago.

Healing emotionally is a process that requires time, devotion, and understanding. We cannot anticipate an instantaneous recovery, but with the necessary aid and guidance, we can slowly begin to manage our anguish and discover an approach to progress in life.

Jesus proclaimed, "Come to Me, all of you who are weary and burdened, and I will give you rest." (Matthew 11:28 HSCB). This verse speaks to the universal yearning that lies deep in every human heart: the need for rest and relief from the weight of our daily struggles. Whether we are physically exhausted, emotionally drained, or spiritually oppressed, at some point in our lives we all experience weariness and fatigue.

"Come to Me" is an invitation to develop a personal relationship with Jesus Christ where we allow ourselves to receive his love and grace. This relationship brings a sense of security and peace that can be challenging to find amid the chaos of the world. Jesus promises to give us not only physical rest but also spiritual rest—a break from constantly striving and struggling through life. It is an opportunity to release control and submit to his will.

As humans, we are always in pursuit of something—material success, love, or spiritual enlightenment. We yearn for more and constantly strive toward our goals. This also can explain the selfish acts that humans do in order to attain what they desire. But it's important to remember that true rest and peace can only be found in God.

In times of hardship and struggle, it's easy to lose sight of this truth. Even when we have become victims of the selfish acts of others, it's crucial to remember that Jesus is the only one who can provide us with true rest. We must remind ourselves to turn to Him for comfort and guidance and trust that He will lead us toward fulfillment.

Through these words, he was telling us that if we seek him out for help and strength during our times of difficulty, he will be there. In the same way, when dealing with emotional wounds or embarking on a healing journey, we can turn to Jesus for guidance and solace every step of the way.

Emotional wounds can have a serious impact on our mental health. When we experience emotional pain, it can leave us feeling overwhelmed, isolated, and anxious. In some cases, the effects of emotional wounds can be long-lasting and debilitating.

In order to truly understand the impact of emotional wounds on our mental health, we must first acknowledge that these wounds often stem from unresolved conflicts in our past. These conflicts can range from deeply traumatic experiences to childhood neglect or abuse or even minor misunderstandings with those closest to us. Regardless of their origin, emotional wounds have the potential to induce feelings of guilt, shame, depression, and anxiety. By recognizing the source of our emotional pain, we can begin to take the necessary steps toward healing and freeing ourselves from the weight of the past.

It is also important to understand that although these emotions can be hard to deal with, they are not permanent and can be overcome with the right help. Building a strong support system is essential for anyone dealing with emotional wounds. Developing healthy relationships with family, friends, and professionals can provide us with a valuable perspective on how we process our emotions. Seeking professional help from counselors or therapists can also give us the opportunity to learn the skills and strategies we need to heal our emotional wounds.

It is also important to remember that healing takes time and should be done with patience and self-compassion. Taking care of our mental health can help us move forward in life, despite the difficult emotions we may feel as a result of past experiences. Understanding, accepting, and managing our emotions can help us create a more positive outlook and lead a healthier, happier life.

Ultimately, it is important to remember that even though we may carry these wounds for many years, there is hope for healing and growth. We all have the capacity to heal from emotional pain and create meaningful relationships with those around us. It is never too late to start the journey of healing, and with patience, self-compassion, and professional help, we can find our way toward emotional wellness.

Emotional wounds come in many shapes and sizes, and each of us carries them differently. Feelings of abandonment, rejection, betrayal, guilt, shame, and low self-esteem are some of the most common types. But no matter the form they take, they all share one thing in common: the power to hold us back.

Abandonment and rejection can cause deep emotional wounds, leaving us feeling disconnected, alone, and unheard. Abandonment may stem from feeling neglected or left behind by important people in our lives, leading to a fear of not being accepted or heard. Rejection can manifest as being turned away, ignored, or dismissed by those we hold dear, leading to struggles with trust, sensitivity to criticism, and difficulty forming meaningful relationships.

Both betrayal and guilt carry heavy and complex feelings. They also hold immense power. Betrayal usually involves someone who has broken the trust between them and another person. Signs of betrayal may include difficulty trusting people, feeling betrayed and damaged, and a fear of being hurt again. Guilt is an internal battle between our conscience and our actions. It often involves feelings of regret or remorse when we feel like we've done something wrong or hurtful to someone else.

Betrayal is a powerful violation of trust that can devastate the most ancient and loyal of relationships. It can appear in many forms, such as difficulty trusting others, intense feelings of betrayal and apprehension, and fear of being hurt anew. Yet in conquering these emotions, we can ascend to greater power over our own lives and open up exciting paths for discovering deeper insight into how we interact with one another. By doing so, we can gain a greater knowledge of the very essence of ourselves and understand even more profoundly who we are. Believing that greater appreciation for our relationships may emerge, creating a silver lining of potential despite an overwhelming feeling of despair.

Guilt is an internal battle that we face when our actions do not align with our conscience. It involves feelings of regret and remorse when we hurt someone else. It may be an internal battle, but it is an opportunity to reflect and acknowledge how our choices have hurt another. This internal unrest motivated by guilt can bring about reflection and meaningful change to ensure we make the best choices next time, particularly when those choices may potentially hurt someone else. In such moments, we have the capacity to learn how to uprightly prioritize others' needs over our own as well as how to take responsibility by owning up with real sincerity.

Shame is a powerful emotion that can make us feel small, humiliated, embarrassed, unworthy, and insignificant. It can make us feel inadequate and unworthy of love and acceptance. It's that voice in our head that tells us we're not good enough, that we don't measure up to the standards others hold, and that we don't deserve love or acceptance. Low self-esteem can lead to a vicious cycle of negative thinking, which can further exacerbate shame and feelings of worthlessness.

But here's the thing: shame and low self-esteem are only as powerful as we allow them to be. We have the power to overcome shame and low self-esteem! We have the power to rise above our feelings of worthlessness, helplessness, and hopelessness. We have the power to break this cycle and take control of our lives.

We all deserve love and acceptance, even if that is not something we can find from those around us. Recognizing this worthiness within ourselves is where it starts, irrespective of the opinions and judgments levied by others. This is an opportunity for every one of us to question what it truly means to be worthy of lifelong love. We must make space for appreciation in our lives that goes beyond the expectations set out by society because we deserve a unique brand of affection that originates within ourselves.

We may feel constantly burdened by our flaws and imperfections, but at the same time, it's important to recognize that these imperfections compose a great part of what forms us. They shape us into who we are and contribute to our individuality. By learning how to adopt a healthier outlook toward these elements, we can discover a way of seeing their value rather than focusing on their shortcomings. To embrace them is to dive deep into ourselves and tap into previously unrecognized strength, which leads to growth both internally and externally. Our quirks and idiosyncrasies make us unique; they testify to the unwritten story written uniquely within each of us that compels and empowers! To truly accept ourselves is the first step toward unlocking an untold potential—our truest power lies in true self-acceptance.

So the next time you feel shame creeping in, remember this: you are more than your mistakes, your failures, and your shortcomings. You are a complex, multifaceted human being with endless potential and infinite worth. So stand tall, hold your head up high, and never let shame hold you back from living your best life.

When we are hurt, it can be challenging to forgive; however, understanding why taking the path of understanding allows us to journey to complete and whole healing is essential for our emotional well-being. Unforgiveness creates an unwelcoming cell, a joint of bitterness, which traps us in a continuous space of feeling hostile or infuriated. Through not forgiving we stop ourselves from maturing or developing and ceasing our growth.

Additionally, blocking off or avoiding forgiving others could potentially impact our physical health—any bitterness we hold contributes to irrational levels of unnecessary stress and discomfort on top of the pain that was first experienced itself. The blocks that are created when we refuse to forgive can have a significant impact on our physical, mental, and spiritual health. The Bible speaks of bitterness as an indication of the hurt and suffering we carry, which can affect our core being over time. It also speaks of the root of bitterness as a sign of spiritual sickness and warns us to seek out God's healing when we are in this state. Taking on the practice of forgiveness offers an essential opportunity for emotional, spiritual, and physical healing. This can be achieved through accepting our circumstances and actively choosing not to hold negative views about the person or situation that has caused us hurt.

Creating healthier relationships is an important part of addressing emotional wounds. This means learning how to express yourself honestly and openly, and how to recognize the needs of both you and others. It also means learning how to effectively manage conflict, set healthy boundaries, and communicate in ways that make it easier for you to be heard. Working with a therapist can help you develop these skills so that your relationships will become healthier and more fulfilling.

In addition, healing emotional wounds often requires a willingness to confront and explore the underlying issues that have caused them. This means facing difficult memories and emotions and developing insight into how they have shaped your thoughts and behaviors in the present. With guidance from a qualified mental health professional, you can learn how to identify destructive patterns that may be preventing you from moving forward, and how to process painful experiences in a safe and supportive environment.

By working patiently and diligently through powerful processes of deep self-exploration and healing, you can begin to unravel the pain and struggles of your past for a healthier, more meaningful future. Perseverance and conscientiousness are foundational tenets of emotional healing, but time is needed for many people to directly reference meaningful change in their lives. Despite the inherent obstacles each person often faces in neutralizing debilitating tempers from a painful past, it's possible to place greater precedence on promising hopes for your future.

Emotional wounds are not always visible to the naked eye, but their impact can be just as debilitating as physical injuries. These wounds are the result of past experiences that have left us hurt and scared, and they often manifest themselves in the form of anxiety, depression, and addiction. However, identifying these hidden wounds is the first step toward healing and regaining control over our lives.

It takes courage and the willingness to confront our past, but the rewards are immeasurable. By uncovering and addressing emotional wounds, we can break free from the chains of our past and finally experience the peace and happiness that we deserve. So let's take that first step, together, toward healing and liberation.

Reflection Questions

1. How do I typically respond to emotional wounds? Do I tend to suppress or ignore them, or do I actively work to address them?

2. What are some of the emotional wounds that I have experienced in my life? How have they impacted my thoughts, emotions, and behaviors?

3. How can I differentiate between an emotional wound and a temporary emotional response to a situation?

4. What are some of the negative beliefs or patterns that I have developed as a result of my emotional wounds? How can I work to change these beliefs or patterns?

5. What strategies can I use to help me uncover and process my emotional wounds in a healthy and effective way?

WE ARE GOD'S MASTERPIECES:
Understanding *Our* Emotions

"I will praise You, for I am fearfully and wonderfully made. Marvelous are Your works, And that my soul knows very well." Psalm 139:14 (NKJV)

The chapter discusses the idea that as God's masterpiece, we have the ability to forgive others. It explains that because we are made in the image of a loving God, we also have the capacity to love and forgive. Forgiveness can be a difficult task, but it is made possible through reliance on God's strength. The chapter emphasizes the importance of forgiveness, as unforgiveness can cause long-term emotional damage and keep us stuck in negative emotions. The power of forgiveness is liberating and can help us build stronger relationships and bring peace into our lives. The chapter concludes by reminding readers that we are all God's masterpieces and have been given the gift of forgiveness.

In the Bible, we are often referred to as God's workmanship. He has taken us—broken and flawed human beings—and crafted something beautiful out of it. While there is still work to be done in our lives, every day we see progress being made through the grace of Jesus Christ. As a result, we can approach each day with the hope and purpose of being crafted into something beautiful. We are considered the apex of God's creation. God sees us as a work of art. His grace is sufficient to shape and mold us into a masterpiece— the person He created us to be. We can have assurance knowing that, in spite of all odds, we have been called out by God to be something special.

He is the Master Craftsman, and we are His masterpieces. We are not just pieces of clay to be molded into whatever shape God desires; rather, we are intricately woven together with love and care. With each passing day, our transformation continues until we reach a place of perfection.

At times, we may feel incapable of living a life that truly honors God. However, in those moments, we can remind ourselves of the remarkable transformation that is happening within us. We have been granted the capacity to forgive, love unconditionally, shift our thinking, and live out our lives in the overflow of God's grace. Harnessing these abilities will not always be easy, but we must persevere. Only then can we embrace the incredible transformation that is taking place within us and live our lives more meaningfully.

It is a gift from God that we have been called to be His workmanship and that He continues to shape us into something more beautiful than we could ever imagine. We can rejoice in the knowledge that even though our emotions may sometimes seem overwhelming, we are being refined by a loving and merciful God who desires to make us whole.

We are God's masterpiece, and as such we have the ability to forgive others. This is because when we are made in the image of a loving God, we also have the capacity to love and forgive just as He does. To be able to fully understand what it means for us to be God's masterpiece and therefore be capable of forgiving others is a tremendous gift. This connection enables us to look beyond our own pain and hurt and instead choose mercy and grace in order to heal ourselves and the relationship between the two parties. Forgiveness is not an easy task, but it is possible through reliance on God's strength so that we can move forward with Him in our lives. Being God's masterpiece gives us the courage to forgive, so we can be free from the hurts and pains of the past and move forward into a future full of hope, joy, and peace. We should never forget that we are indeed His masterpieces and have been given this tremendous gift of forgiveness.

We all experience emotional hurt and pain at some point in our lives, but it is important to understand that unforgiveness can be the root cause of long-term, deep emotional damage. Unforgiveness keeps us stuck in a cycle of negative emotions—such as anger, bitterness, or resentment—which prevents us from moving forward and creating a healthier and happier life.

The Bible says this about unforgiveness: "Get rid of all bitterness, rage and anger, brawling and slander, along with every form of malice. Be kind and compassionate to one another..." (Ephesians 4:31-32 NIV). Often, when an offense occurs in our lives and we don't forgive, it can create an emotional weight that can be hard to carry. But when we choose to forgive, something miraculous happens—we are set free from the burden of bitterness. Forgiving others not only sets us free but also strengthens our relationships, releasing us from the inner prison that comes from the hurt we feel.

Every experience you've had since birth left an imprint on the fabric of your life. Some experiences from childhood are difficult to remember just as some are easy to recall. Some of the more difficult or traumatic experiences are generally repressed but triggered by certain events or circumstances. Our past experiences can shape our outlook on life in an unhealthy way if we allow them to do so. Each experience had the potential to build you up or tear you down, depending on what happened. You may be familiar with the saying that forgiving someone is equivalent to forgetting their offense. It is important to recognize that forgiving someone doesn't necessarily mean forgetting what happened or granting permission for the offense to continue. It does, however, require making a conscious choice to let go of negative feelings and focus on grace and mercy instead. Forgiveness requires vulnerability and courage, and it is not always easy—but it can be one of the most beautiful gifts we give to others and ourselves.

As previously mentioned, forgiveness isn't synonymous with weakness; instead, it embodies strength. It can be incredibly difficult, but it is also incredibly powerful. Forgiveness is not a calling only given to Christians, yet for those who follow the teachings of Christ, it should be viewed as a central element of their faith. We may come across hardships in our lives and find it incredibly difficult to go against selfish desires and forgive. However, this capacity holds immense strength; forgiving others requires strength within us that can set off tremendous acts of healing, growth, and an intensity of love that cannot be shared or expressed through words. Going against human nature can make you feel powerless, but forgiveness will lead to profound freedom.

Learning to adjust expectations can also be a major factor in healing emotional wounds. This is because it helps us accept our circumstances rather than become frustrated or overwhelmed by them. By having realistic expectations, we are able to focus on what is within our control, allowing us to make constructive changes that can lead to healthier outcomes. Adjusting our expectations also allows us to focus on what we can do rather than ruminate on what we cannot.

Learning to let go can be an important part of healing emotional wounds. By letting go of expectations, needs, and desires that are not achievable or realistic, we can free ourselves from the burden of frustration or disappointment. This allows us to focus on the present moment, which can bring us peace and clarity. Letting go also helps us accept our current situation and has the potential to bring us joy and contentment. Contentment is an essential element in healing emotional wounds. Contentment is a peaceful state of mind where we learn to acknowledge our existing circumstances and take pleasure in the present moments. How does this apply to learning to forgive? The Bible says that in order to receive contentment, we must first forgive. When we choose to forgive and let go of negative feelings, a sense of peace and joy can arise, paving the way to emotional healing.

We can start the process of emotional healing by forgiving, managing our expectations, and releasing negative emotions. We can learn to accept our circumstances and take pleasure in the present moment, which is the foundation of true contentment. No matter how deep the hurt or how difficult it may be, we can make the conscious choice to forgive and open ourselves up to a new beginning. When we forgive, we can finally be set free from the emotional pain of our past and enjoy a life of freedom. The Bible encourages us to bear with one another, forgive one another, and to be able to extend mercy and grace. By living out these words of encouragement, we can find true contentment and genuine healing.

Learning to forgive ourselves is a critical step in healing emotional wounds. By accepting our mistakes and learning from them, we can move forward with more compassion and understanding for ourselves. Forgiveness can also provide relief from guilt or shame that may have been associated with a particular event, allowing us to be more open and accepting of our own emotions.

Ultimately, healing emotional wounds is an ongoing process that requires dedication and commitment. By developing greater awareness of our emotions, adjusting expectations, letting go of what we cannot control, and learning to forgive ourselves for past mistakes, we can begin the journey toward emotional healing.

Forgiveness is not easy, but avoiding it takes an even higher toll on our emotional and spiritual well-being. Unforgiveness destroys our relationship with God and keeps us in a prison of bitterness, anger, and despair. It can lead to physical illnesses, emotional pain, and spiritual darkness. The longer we carry the burden of unforgiveness in our hearts, the more it takes a toll on our lives. When we choose to forgive those who have hurt us, we free ourselves from the prison of unforgiveness and instead take hold of God's gift of grace and mercy. We can choose to live in the joy of God's love rather than the bondage of unforgiveness.

God has created us as His masterpiece with an amazing capacity for both love and forgiveness. When we realize this truth, we can trust in Him to give us the strength and courage to forgive those who have hurt us, and to live in freedom. Let us take this opportunity to forgive so that we can be the masterpiece God created us to be.

Forgiveness is a powerful gift from God. It sets us free from the pain of unforgiveness and brings healing and restoration into our lives and allows us to step into our calling and purpose as we continue our walk with God. Forgiveness is a vehicle that forces us to grow and become the masterpiece He has created us to be. As human beings, we often struggle to navigate the complexities of our emotions. It can be challenging to understand why we feel the way we do and how to respond to those feelings appropriately. However, as God's masterpiece, we have been uniquely created with the ability to experience a vast range of emotions.

As human beings, we possess a remarkable gift: emotions. But why did God give us the ability to feel so deeply? Each emotion holds a unique purpose, whether to signal us of danger or to move us to act in a certain way. When we are overcome with joy, it can inspire us to spread that positivity to others. When we experience sadness, we can learn to empathize with others and cultivate compassion. There is no denying that emotions can be intense and overwhelming at times, but it is important to remember that they serve a vital role in our lives. You are fearfully and wonderfully made. Yes, you! Your unique qualities, talents, and emotions are all beautiful parts of who you are. You were created with purpose and intention by a loving God who holds you in the palm of His hand.

Life is full of highs and lows, but each and every moment is a testament to your faith in Him and your resilience. Trust that God will give you the strength you need to face whatever comes your way. Remember that you are not alone on this journey. So embrace all that makes you who you are and let God guide you through it all. You were made for something special. Don't give up, keep pushing forward, and watch as your purpose unfolds before your very eyes.

Reflection Questions

1. How do I typically approach my emotions? Do I tend to suppress them, or do I allow myself to fully experience and process them?

2. What emotions am I currently experiencing related to a specific situation or experience? How are these emotions impacting my thoughts and behaviors?

3. How can understanding ourselves as God's masterpieces help us to forgive others?

4. What are some examples of negative emotions that can result from unforgiveness, and how do they affect our lives?

5. How can relying on God's strength help us to forgive others when it may seem impossible to do so on our own?

HEALING FROM THE PAST:
Overcoming Deep Emotional Wounds
Caused *by* Unforgiveness

*"I have seen his ways, but I will heal him; I will lead him
and restore comfort to him and his mourners, creating
words of praise." The Lord says, "Peace, peace to the one
who is far or near, and I will heal him."*
Isaiah 57:18–19 (HSCB)

In this chapter, we will discuss how to transform our past experiences into lessons. We'll look at the importance of accepting and understanding our emotions as well as changing our thought patterns and behavior. Additionally, we will explore different ways to cope with feelings of guilt and shame so that we can begin to heal from emotional wounds.

What if others could view your emotional wounds just as clearly as we can see the jewelry, clothing, shoes, and hairstyle that you wear? Would you feel confident or ashamed? As humans, we often attempt to hide our emotional pain and insecurities behind a mask of perfection. We attempt to conceal our pain by putting on smiles, laughing, and pretending to be fine.

This was the reality for one minister who, for years, walked with a mask of perfection and an abundance of pride. He grew up in a home where he experienced abuse from his father, and although he had become a successful minister, his childhood experience caused him to carry unforgiveness in his heart.

This unforgiveness led him to make decisions that impacted his relationship with his son, and when the truth was revealed after a heated argument, his son could not understand how his father could be so unforgiving and hurtful. The minister's mask was finally shattered, and he was forced to face the truth—he allowed his unforgiveness and pain from childhood abuse to control his life and relationships.

It was in that moment of truth and clarity that the minister realized he had to make a choice. He could choose to stay stuck in the pain of his past or choose to let go of his unforgiveness and embrace truth, forgiveness, and freedom.

The complexity of this story lies in the fact that it takes a considerable amount of courage and strength to let go of unforgiveness and choose to forgive. This story speaks to the very real struggle that many go through in their lifetime—the struggle between discomfort and fear and the courage it takes to choose freedom from the past. This story speaks of the power of truth and forgiveness and how it can set you free from the chains that have bound you for years.

Forgiveness is a profound and challenging concept to comprehend, but the rewards it brings are immeasurable. Carrying the weight of past hurts and grievances can cause deep emotional wounds that can linger for years or even lifetimes. However, it's crucial to recognize that these wounds go beyond mere hurt feelings. Rather, they are complex issues that affect our mental health, spiritual life, and overall well-being.

An unforgiving attitude can cause a person to feel isolated, anxious, and depressed. We carry these wounds with us, preventing us from fully engaging in life. Unless we take steps to forgive, our wounds may prevent us from forming and maintaining meaningful relationships. We may be unable to accept and receive God's love or the love of others.

Some wounds are so deep that it feels like they go straight to the core of our very being. Unforgiveness can cause a type of pain that can persist, extending far beyond the moment of its inception, and may follow us until the very end, unless we choose the path of release and let go. We desperately search for a solution to move away from this hurt, but all paths seem blocked by an invisible force. The journey of healing may feel almost impossible in this state, and pessimism creeps up when we don't see progress.

Unforgiveness is an emotion that spreads like wildfire, stifling and trapping us in a life without true freedom. The weight of holding on to anger and resentment only brings more pain, conflicts, and distress into our lives. Such strong and resentful emotions can easily corrupt the spirit, draining our inner peace and causing growing pains within. This unwavering bitterness toward what had been done before becomes a tangible weight that impedes your ability to just live joyfully and risk to trust again, one that begets nothing but turmoil. In burrowing deep, overlooking, and refusing to accept the moments of hurt, we become shackled by our own disdain, left yearning for a deliverance, which only comes with letting go.

Unforgiveness is the inability or unwillingness to forgive, having or making no allowance for error or weakness. What circumstance(s) would make us unwilling or unable to forgive another person? Can we say that we are completely without any error or fault and that we have never done anything to harm another person? Why is it so hard to forgive?

The answer to these questions can be found in the Scriptures. The Bible speaks of a God who is slow to anger and abounding in love (Psalm 103:8). He also instructs us to forgive as we have been forgiven (Ephesians 4:32). According to Romans 3:23 (KJV), "For all have sinned, and come short of the glory of God." We are all imperfect, and because of this, we need to be forgiven. We have a responsibility to one another, and we are called to forgive. We should extend the same level of mercy and grace that we expect to receive. This verse speaks to the fundamental human condition of imperfection and fallibility. It reminds us that as human beings, we are prone to error and sin and that we all fall short of the perfection and glory of God. This is a central idea in Christian theology, which emphasizes the concept of original sin and the need for redemption through Jesus Christ.

From a philosophical perspective, this verse highlights the tension between human imperfection and the ideal of perfection. The concept of perfection is a central idea in many philosophical traditions, from Plato's theory of Forms to the Aristotelian idea of the perfect state[18]. However, the reality of human existence is one of imperfection and limitation. We are finite beings with finite abilities, and we are subject to the frailties and limitations of the human condition.

The recognition of our own imperfection is a crucial step toward humility and self-awareness. It reminds us that we are not God and that we must rely on divine grace and guidance in order to live a fulfilling and meaningful life. It also emphasizes the importance of forgiveness and compassion, both toward us and toward others who also fall short of the ideal.

Forgiveness can be hard to give and may seem arduous, but it is essential that we do in fact give it. We must be cognizant of the fact that forgiveness serves as an act of obedience toward our heavenly Father and a glistening representation of the love He comprises for us. If we relish how much the Lord has pardoned us for our wrongdoings, which abound, then we shall find ourselves grateful for life with newfound enthusiasm to forgive those who have

---

[18] Fine, Gail. *On Ideas: Aristotle's Criticism of Plato's Theory of Forms*. Kindle. Vol. 104. New York, United States of America: Oxford University Press, 1995. https://doi.org/10.2307/2186014.

damaged us along our journey through life. Never forget all that God has given, done, and pardoned us from in full appreciation as you discover your capacity and devotion to forgive others as time elapses.

Harnessing the power to forgive and let go of anger and resentment toward others can be truly freeing and liberating. It opens our hearts and minds—taking us away from darkness, bitterness, and grudges in exchange for lightness, understanding, and resiliency. With it we can unlock gateways leading to an unyielding wellspring of love, hope, and kindness while simultaneously making way for reflection, transformation, and healing. In other words, forgiveness is a power that can make us feel strong and happy. We can forgive people and stop feeling angry or unhappy. Forgiveness helps us to be kind, hopeful, and loving. It also helps us to learn from what happened and heal our hearts.

Just as our willingness and ability to forgive those around us is a manifestation of God's love *in* us, it is also a reflection of His love *for* us. When we can look past the wrongs done by others and show forgiveness, it shows that we understand what it means to have been forgiven by God. When we take the initiative to forgive, we are allowing God's grace and mercy to be seen in our lives. We all make mistakes that require forgiveness from others—even ourselves. We can experience true freedom when we choose to let go of unforgiveness and embrace a heart of forgiveness toward those who have aggrieved, offended, or hurt us. Furthermore, when we choose to forgive, it can be a powerful means of restoring relationships.

Forgiveness is not easy; it takes time and effort. We must take the time to reflect on our own wrongs, evaluate our relationships, and reestablish trust. According to Matthew 18:21–22, we are encouraged to forgive others not only seven times but up to seventy-seven (77) times. What does this imply? It means that we are to forgive without limit. We must put our pride aside and choose to be humble servants of the Lord, taking on His character of mercy and grace. It is important to have the willingness to forgive both major wrongs and minor offenses. This is an incredibly hard task; however, it is possible through the power of God's grace. When we hold on to unforgiveness in our hearts, it can have a detrimental effect on us both mentally and spiritually. It robs us of joy, causes distrust and resentment in our relationships, and can lead to bitterness. But when we choose to practice forgiveness, it brings healing and freedom for both the offender and the offended. It also allows us to experience a deeper sense of grace from God and tap into a different level of peace.

The effects of unforgiveness can sometimes have deadly consequences. We often see in news headlines where violence is promulgated as a result of an offense that has gone unaddressed. Forgiveness can only be possible when we understand what forgiveness is about. Even now, people are suffering from deep emotional wounds because of unforgiveness. Some individuals have been injured mentally, physically, emotionally and just simply existing but concealed among the crowd. They are left standing in the shadow of hurt. As a result, life is not a reality but a surreal experience, a never-ending chain of events that have been somewhat disconnected from one another. Those individuals suffer and never seem to find peace within.

Forgiveness allows you to take off the damaged goods label. It allows you to stop thinking about the mistakes you made, who hurt you, and what did not work out for you. God knows every person who has offended you or treated you unfairly, every struggle, every bad break. He has promised that if you remain in faith, He will repay you for the trouble and pain you've had to undergo. He will repay you double for the unfair things that have occurred.

Now, this is not to suggest that there is some special blanket to cover or wand to wave in the air to dismiss all the wrong that has been done to cause the issue to just go away or mysteriously vanish, but it is to bring you to a place of inner peace in God, assured that nothing under the sun is hidden and that He has the last word on for your life. He is sovereign and will judge what is good and right accordingly. If we can identify the root cause of the pain beyond the surface or cloak of the incident, then we can decide to activate the power of forgiveness which requires work that will ultimately lead to the release needed to experience freedom.

Mark 11:25–26 (RSV) says, "And whenever you stand praying, forgive, if you have anything against anyone, so that your Father also who is in heaven may forgive you your trespasses." This is essential in maintaining a relationship with God. Also, we are encouraged to forgive so that we can receive the gift of forgiveness, so the process becomes twofold. Cleansing ourselves in this matter also allows the opportunity to steer clear of the root of bitterness which is self-destructive and has the propensity for long-lasting consequences. The Bible speaks of the root of bitterness as being unproductive, a poison to the soul, and even contagious. There are also spiritual ties to unforgiveness and the root of bitterness. Demonic spirits attached to unforgiveness are a breeding ground for disease, depression, and anxiety. Forgiveness is the key to breaking free from their grip. Forgiveness makes us free. It increases our faith, brings us into unity with God, and cleanses us from the spiritual pollution of bitterness. Like a heavy load being taken off our backs, forgiveness frees us from the destructive effects of unresolved anger. It creates space for understanding and reconciliation. When we forgive, we are allowing God to work in our lives and make things right. We can let go of any ill feelings we have toward the person who aggrieved, offended, or hurt us and trust that God will act on our behalf. In doing this, we can experience the freedom of being fully alive in Christ, unencumbered by the weight of unforgiveness and bitterness. We can be sure that God will deal with any wrongs done against us in His time, and we can be comforted in knowing that God is sovereign and will bring justice, peace, and healing. Forgiveness is an act of grace and mercy, and it brings a sense of peace and joy as we allow God to work in our hearts.

Are we, as humans, all equipped with an innate ability to forgive? We may find this capacity tested every day. Unforgiveness is a state of not carrying that ability any further. It can present itself in various capacities such as a refusal, inaction, or intention to not attribute any leniency whatsoever. Its presence restricts us from dreaming of a brighter future and blocks out the floodgates of our potential to progress. We must summon the strength within ourselves to pardon—to keep love in our hearts and forgiveness on our lips so humanity can take flight toward total kindness and generosity.

Unforgiveness is a heavy burden although often overlooked. It can take many forms, leaving the one who bears it feeling powerless and prisoner to their own destructive thoughts. We may direct unforgiveness outwardly toward others, expressing anger or hurt, or even toward ourselves inwardly, deepening our self-hatred and shame. Regardless of the direction it takes, if unchecked, it contaminates our soul.

It is essential for us to recognize and release all feelings of unforgiveness so that we can free ourselves from hostility and forgive those we feel wronged by—mercifully, allowing us the opportunity for growth instead of withering away inside a cloying mist of unresolved agony. By honestly making peace with our story, whether by finding purpose in the pain or striving to reconcile differences, we create space in which love and understanding can enter—not only within our internal landscape, but also with those around us producing powerful ripples of transformation that are felt across systems both big and small!

Unforgiveness can lead to a chain reaction of unfortunate effects on our mental and physical health. Amplified stress levels, chronic inflammation, depression, anxiety, and sleeping problems are just some of the results accomplished by breaking down our psyches with unforgiveness. Our immune system is also weakened, as is our delicate digestive system, producing more negativity and illness within us. But that's not all. We bring it into life around us, striating interpersonal relationships, hindering work productivity, and tainting the important ability to produce a quality of life in shared moments with those we care about most.

Unforgiveness can stem from a variety of situations, such as trauma or abuse, betrayal by a loved one, a long-term hurt, unresolved feelings of anger and resentment, a lack of remorse or accountability on the part of the person who hurt them, or personal values or beliefs that make it difficult to forgive.

It's important to understand that forgiveness is a personal process, and it may take time. It's also important to recognize that forgiveness does not mean forgetting what happened or that the hurt or betrayal was okay. It's about letting go of negative emotions and moving on from the hurt.

Additionally, when we fail to process our past emotional hurt and avoid seeking out ways to cope with it, it may also open the door for us to connect it to current situations. This can cause us to react disproportionately to current situations, leading to an overgeneralization of past hurt to current situations and people.

Furthermore, unresolved past emotional hurt can lead to the formation of negative beliefs such as "I am not worthy of love" or "people will always hurt me," which can shape the way a person perceives and interprets experiences in the present, leading to further connection to past hurt.

It is important to understand that connecting past emotional hurt to current situations can create a cycle of negative thoughts, feelings, and behaviors that could affect your ability to enjoy life.

Your emotions can keep you in bondage with bitterness and unforgiveness if you don't deal with them properly. The reality is that it is impossible to completely let go of the past when it comes to emotions. If you wait to forgive until you feel like it, you will never actually forgive and will continue to experience negative effects. In the intricate mosaic of our existence, we uncover a profound trinity: the mind, the heart, and the soul. Our mind is where we gain knowledge and understanding, while our heart is where we experience emotions. Forgiveness starts with our will, which is found in our soul—the part of us where we make decisions. When we forgive, we are deciding on the will to move forward and release the emotional burden that comes with being hurt.

The past has a way of holding us with an unyielding grip, even when we keenly desire to move on. Deep emotional wounds from unforgiveness can weigh us down like a ton of bricks, hindering us from experiencing true inner peace. Healing from such wounds can be arduous and demanding, but it is a necessary journey if one is to experience genuine freedom. To heal, we must introspectively examine what needs to be released and let go of the emotional baggage that we've been carrying around. It's time to embrace a new, more peaceful future by embracing forgiveness and letting go of the past, thereby unlocking the potential to live life to its fullest.

Reflection Questions

1. What past experiences have been particularly challenging or painful for me? How have these experiences impacted my beliefs and behaviors?

2. How can I reframe past wounds as opportunities for growth and learning? What specific lessons can I draw from these experiences?

3. How can I use self-compassion to forgive myself for mistakes I have made in the past and move forward in a positive way?

4. How can I use my past experiences to empathize with and support others who may be going through similar challenges?

5. What steps can I take to intentionally integrate the lessons that I have learned from my past experiences into my current life and decision-making process?

The Journey *of* Forgiveness: Letting Go to Fulfill Your Purpose

"Be kind to one another, tenderhearted, forgiving one another, as God in Christ forgave you."

Ephesians 4:32 (ESV)

This chapter explores the connection between forgiveness and fulfilling one's purpose in life. The chapter emphasizes that forgiveness is not only important for our own well-being and healing but also for living a fulfilling life. It offers a spiritual perspective on forgiveness, emphasizing that forgiveness is not only a human act but also an act of grace and a reflection of God's love and mercy. Ultimately, the chapter encourages readers to embrace forgiveness as a key component of their spiritual journey and a means of fulfilling God's purpose for their lives.

Our lives are intertwined in ways that can be difficult to explain. It's as if our stories overlap and become one, even though we may never meet or even know of each other's existence. We are connected by the intangible threads of shared humanity—moments we've both experienced, feelings we've both had, and memories that have been made and will never be forgotten. This interconnection is what binds us all together, and it's the foundation of our shared journey through life. No matter our backgrounds, beliefs, or circumstances, we all face similar struggles, challenges, and times of happiness along the way.

We experience hurt daily, and for some, this becomes internalized and processed into rejection, causing massive damage in some cases. Some examples of this hurt can come from family, friends, work, or even a traumatic event. Our responses to each of these situations and how we process those events are influenced by our mental and emotional capacity as well as our personal perspective. It can also be influenced by our own set of beliefs and how we have been conditioned to respond to situations. Studies have shown that when we don't process our hurt, it can become a source of resentment, judgment, and anger. Forgiveness is the best remedy to this hurt. It sets us free from the bondage of resentment and bitterness, allowing us to move forward with peace, joy, and freedom.

Forgiveness can be straightforward with an apology from the offender and the victim's willingness to forgive. However, at times it can be an extremely difficult task, regardless of the time of day or level of apology. The effects of the offense can be too much to handle, and some never recover, while others bear scars that never seem to fade away.

There are individuals who are still carrying the burden of past offenses from people who have passed away. The sad part is, they are held hostage by the rage and bitterness they feel from an offense that occurred that they have not been able to move beyond, and it spills out in their words and sometimes their actions. The path of destruction is largely visible as they become masters of sabotage, leaving a trail of damaged relationships and broken people in their path.

Some individuals turn their pain inward and commit reckless acts that could potentially hurl them headfirst down a dark path. Regardless of whether they seek counseling or other treatment procedures, there is a deep wound that remains because forgiveness can never be enough for them.

We often struggle to disconnect the event and experience from who we are, which creates an internal conflict. The cycle is the same in each case where there is an offense or negative experience that produces a response or reaction. The response or reaction becomes internalized and turns into a deep pain that grows inside, feeding off the energy. It grows more and more with reflection and anything used to remind us of the experience. This cycle repeats itself over and over; it grows, darkens, separates, and repeats. This cycle continues until you are deeply rooted in bitterness and hatred.

We can't afford to live in the place of offense. Learning how to let go is a personal process, and sometimes it is not easy to forgive, especially in situations of severe betrayal, trauma, or abuse. It's important to understand that forgiveness should be immediate although the process of healing, and trust takes time. It is okay to allow yourself time as necessary while processing as long as the end result is to forgive.

Letting go creates the basic starting point for any relationship that has gone bad and provides the space to experience emotional freedom. It is an extremely powerful force as it brings a broader perspective to a damaged relationship. A great part of forgiveness is initially forgiving oneself. This becomes a continued struggle, and the damage is evident as relationships are shattered, marriages are dissolved, and people are either incarcerated or lives are lost due to the inability to forgive. Total forgiveness is essential and possible, providing healing from deep emotional wounds, though it provides a challenge. Forgiveness serves as a reminder to consider a person as a whole rather than just focusing on their wrongful actions, even when they have caused harm to someone else. It can become easier to let go when we understand that everyone makes mistakes at some point or another and no one is perfect. Acknowledging these facts may be hard, yet it fosters a sense of understanding and compassion. Looking at the offense can be extremely painful; however, embracing forgiveness can open up one's heart to loving feelings again and foster healthier relationships. As previously discussed, granting forgiveness to someone doesn't mean you overlook their actions or justify their misconduct. Instead, it's about coming to terms with the circumstances and liberating yourself from the burden of negative feelings.

Overcoming resistance to forgiveness starts with identifying the feelings of anger and hurt that need to be released. This process may take time and patience, but it will allow for a more peaceful state of mind. Continuing to practice forgiveness can lead to a healthier, more enjoyable life. Letting go can be a difficult process, but ultimately it is worth the effort and brings with it an immense sense of peace. It is important to remember that forgiveness isn't just for others; holding on to anger or resentment toward ourselves can also be damaging. It is possible to find a place of solace and inner peace even as we navigate the challenges of interpersonal relationships and the conflicts they bring.

The Bible teaches that God is a forgiving God who offers forgiveness to all who repent and turn to Him. Forgiveness is at the heart of God's plan for humanity, and it is through forgiveness that we can experience salvation and eternal life. As believers, we are called to reflect God's forgiving nature by forgiving others. God's purpose for our existence is to glorify Him and His love by showing grace, mercy, and forgiveness toward others.

The Bible teaches us that we are commanded to forgive others (Matthew 6:12–15) and that this is not optional. When we forgive others, it reflects God's character of justice and mercy. It also demonstrates our faith in God's power to deliver justice and demonstrate mercy. We have a responsibility to treat others with kindness, even when we are offended or hurt by them. Ultimately, we can trust that He will judge justly and bring about restoration in all things (Romans 12:19–21). By forgiving others, we are honoring God and showing His love to those around us. By forgiving, we can move forward in our relationship with the person that aggrieved, offended, or hurt us, or even deepen it. When we forgive others, we are reflecting God's character of grace and mercy and are modeling what it looks like to follow Jesus in a broken world. We are free to choose forgiveness and to release the pain of the past, trusting in God's justice. Through our actions, we can be a living example of His love, grace, and mercy. Genesis 1:26–28 (NKJV) reveals that human beings were created by God in His image and given a special purpose.

> *26 And God said, Let us make man in our image, after our likeness: and let them have dominion over the fish of the sea, and over the fowl of the air, and over the cattle, and over all the earth, and over every creeping thing that creepeth upon the earth. 27 So God created man in his own image, in the image of God created he him; male and female created he them. 28 And God blessed them, and God said unto them, Be fruitful, and multiply, and replenish the earth, and subdue it: and have dominion over the fish of the sea, and over the fowl of the air, and over every living thing that moveth upon the earth.*

As we look deeper at this scripture, we can see the beginning of creation and the purpose of man. In essence, we were strategically designed and created by God to fulfill a very special purpose. The word "purpose" as defined in Greek is prothesis—or a deliberate plan, proposition, an advance plan, intention/design. It is essential for each one of us to understand that our lives have a purpose, and God already has a plan and design for it. We were not an afterthought but intentionally placed within each unique family and surrounded by those who took the time to mentor, support, and prepare us for this very moment. We should try to overcome the natural instinct of questioning God in times of extreme adversity. God is omniscient, meaning that He knows the beginning from the end. When we are in the midst of pain, it can be difficult to remember or even see this plan, but if we take the time to reflect and be intentional about our thoughts and emotions, we can see God's purpose for us. He has given each one of us the power and capability to live out our purpose. We have to put in the work to understand it and be obedient in following it. God is omnipresent, which means that He is in all places at all times. The Bible teaches in Colossians 1:17 (NKJV) that "He is before all things, and in Him all things consist." Before anything existed, He was there and still holds us together. He is the Alpha and Omega, the beginning and end, our provider and sustainer. We can take comfort in knowing that we are never alone because He is always with us and in Him, everything holds together. When we walk through hard times, remember to focus on God's plan for our lives and His purpose for us. God is omnipotent, which means He is all-powerful. This means that there is nothing too hard for God, and with Him, all things are possible (Matthew 19:26). He created us and sustains us.

We were carefully planted on the earth, so we are like a seed, but because God was responsible for the planting, He is the gardener. As a seed, we are limited in scope and perception. We can only see things through our experience and from the perspective of the seed. Let's explore that concept a bit further. The seed spends nearly its entire cycle surrounded by darkness in a cool, damp restricted isolated environment. In what would seem to be a place where death is imminent, the seed adapts to the environment and begins to grow. It is the job of the gardener to ensure that the seed is placed in a nurturing atmosphere, free of anything that will not contribute to its growth potential. In addition, the gardener tends to the soil that surrounds the seed, creating the necessary environment that will enable the seed to live. Not long after, the seed bursts through the ground, growing into something new and wonderful. God has the responsibility to attend to the needs of the seed, and with proper nourishment and careful attention, it is able to see life as it was meant to be. He provides us with everything we need to thrive and grow spiritually. This helps make sense of the perplexities and complications that seem to overwhelm us and sometimes cause us to stop in our tracks. This does not mean that we will never encounter challenges or difficult times and conflict, but it sets a foundation to understand that we were created for something greater. God has a plan for your life! He already knows that you have particular grace on you and that you have been anointed to fulfill a specific assignment.

Why is this important? Understanding God's purpose for your life can help you find a sense of purpose, compassion, trust, and healing that can aid you in forgiving others. Just as a seed is planted in the ground, it must battle against the elements to eventually bloom into its full potential. Similarly, we are planted in this world by God and must fight against things that challenge our faith to live in our purpose. We are endowed with special gifts from the Lord that give us strength and courage—enabling us to overcome adversity and reach our goals. No matter the hardships and obstacles that come our way, we can rely on

His guidance and grace to help us emerge victorious. Embrace the struggles of life as part of God's plan for your future, and use them as opportunities to grow and develop into who He wants you to be. Understanding God's purpose for your life can help you gain a broader perspective on your situation and the people who have aggrieved, offended, or hurt you. This can help you see the bigger picture and understand that everyone is on their own journey, including those who might have hurt you. It can also help you cultivate compassion toward others.

When you recognize that God has a purpose for everyone, including those who have hurt you, you may feel more empathy toward them and be more willing to forgive them. You can trust that everything happens for a reason and that there is a higher plan at work. This can help you to let go of your hurt and anger toward others and trust that God will work things out in His own way and in His own time. Understanding God's purpose for your life can also help you find healing and peace. When you are able to forgive others, you free yourself from the burden of anger and resentment, which can be incredibly healing. When you are at peace with yourself and with God, you may find that you are better able to move forward with your life and fulfill your own purpose.

When you are assured of your purpose, you're not fearful of people or the external personal conflicts that attempt to strangle you emotionally and strip you of your identity. How could that be the case? It becomes an essential truth to give you the confidence in knowing that sooner or later every issue, obstruction, rival, and opposition in your life will inevitably bow and submit to God's plan and purpose for your life. Why is this important? The hurt that we experience as a result of personal conflicts and interactions can create pain at the deepest emotional and physical levels, and sometimes we become so distorted and mangled that we are unable to find our original shape and design. Our purpose and true design become the center and reference point and knowing that we are ultimately in God's hand.

Forgiveness is a vehicle that allows us to deal with the conflicts that happen from time to time so that we are able to maintain the shape of our purpose and true design despite the unsure realities of conflict and hurt we must endure from time to time without getting stuck in a negative cycle of past hurts. This concept allows us to experience the freedom that we deserve and truly need, which can only come from trusting that God knows our frame and shapes our destiny.

Forgiveness helps us to come out of a hurtful experience as a better version of ourselves, allowing us to see the world with more understanding and less judgment. It teaches us how to love ourselves through understanding and compassion so that we can forgive others for their missteps without resentment or bitterness. Furthermore, it equips us with the tools to forgive ourselves, letting us accept our mistakes and move forward without judgment. By developing our capacity to forgive, we can strengthen our relationships and create more peace in our lives.

Ultimately, forgiveness is an essential part of being human, essential for living a life full of joy and meaning. It gives us the courage to face difficulty with understanding instead of fear and judgment. By understanding the importance and power of forgiveness, we can learn how to handle our relationships and experiences better without getting trapped by our negative emotions. We can learn to create a strong foundation for ourselves that is rooted in compassion and understanding, making it possible for us to live a life filled with love and joy.

Forgiveness is essential to living a life in accordance with God's will. Too often, we allow anger and bitterness to consume our lives, preventing us from fulfilling God's purpose for us. The Bible tells us that we are vessels of His grace and mercy and that when we forgive others, it demonstrates our faithfulness to Him (Colossians 3:13–15).

The power of forgiveness is immense and has the potential to drastically improve our lives in ways we may never have imagined. It can bring peace, healing, and closure to relationships that were once strained or broken. In addition, it helps us break free from the chains of hurtful memories and allows us to put the past behind us.

Forgiveness is not easy, but it's necessary if we want to move forward in our lives and follow God's will. It takes courage and humility to forgive those who have hurt us, but doing so allows us to break free from the cycle of bitterness and resentment that can keep us stuck in the past. It's a choice that requires effort, but it can be immensely rewarding.

When we choose to forgive others, we show God that we trust Him and His plans for our lives—no matter how painful the process of forgiveness may be. This action is not only an act of faithfulness toward Him; it also demonstrates our obedience to His commands. Forgiveness, though it may be hard to practice at times, is a testament to faith and obedience to the Lord. It reflects our duty to trust that He has crafted a plan for us even when we cannot see what lies ahead. When we extend forgiveness to others, it is an act of reverence that reflects the humility and grace of God.

The journey of forgiveness is not an easy path to embark on, but it is a necessary one if we want to fulfill our purpose. Forgiveness requires us to let go of bitterness, anger, and resentment, emotions that can weigh us down and prevent us from moving forward. It involves digging deep and examining our own vulnerabilities and limitations as well as those of others. But by practicing forgiveness, we free ourselves from the burden of negativity and open ourselves up to the possibilities of growth and enlightenment. It is in this space that we can truly begin to fulfill our purpose and lead the life we were meant to live. So let us take this journey together, with an open heart and a willingness to let go, for it is only through forgiveness that we can truly thrive.

Reflection Questions

1. What are some specific ways that forgiveness can help me fulfill God's purpose for my life? How have I experienced this in the past?

2. How can I cultivate a deeper understanding and practice of forgiveness in my daily life, both in my relationship with God and in my interactions with others?

3. How can I let go of the fear and anger that may be preventing me from forgiving those who have hurt me in the past?

DON'T WAIT FOR CLOSURE:
EMBRACE YOUR NEXT CHAPTER
and MOVE FORWARD

"Brethren, I count not myself to have apprehended: but this
one thing I do, forgetting those things which are behind,
and reaching forth unto those things which are before,"
Philippians 3:13 (KJV)

This chapter explores the power of forgiveness and how it can free us from the grip of anger, resentment, and pain. It delves into why it is so important to forgive and let go in order to live a life free from bitterness. Drawing on Bible verses and stories, this chapter encourages readers to embrace forgiveness as a way of releasing negative emotions and restoring peace in their lives. It is a powerful reminder of the importance of forgiving ourselves and others, no matter how difficult it may seem. Through forgiveness, we can free our hearts and find healing.

Embrace your next chapter and move forward without waiting for closure. To begin, you need to forgive yourself. Forgive those who have offended or hurt you and forgive yourself for the mistakes you may have made in the past. It is important to understand that when we let go of hurt and disappointment, we create space for healing. Remember, we are all human and make mistakes.

Once you have forgiven yourself, it's time to let go of the past without needing closure. There are times when we don't receive answers and closure from situations in our lives that leave us feeling incomplete. It can be difficult to move forward without these answers, but it is possible.

When you take time to forgive yourself and move on, your soul will be free of any ties that bind you to a negative space, and you will be able to embrace your next chapter with a clearer and refreshed perspective.

Closure can be elusive, and it doesn't always come when we want or expect it. Instead of waiting for closure that may never come, why not embrace the new chapter that is ahead of you! We are told in Philippians 3:13 to forget the past and look forward to what is ahead. This is a call to action, an invitation from God, to take that step of faith into the next chapter.

When you fully become aware of your purpose and when you let go of expectations for how things are "supposed" to be, you open yourself up to a world of possibilities. You can trust that God is in control and that He will make all things right in His timing. This is important to keep in mind just in case we never get closure or an apology from someone who might have hurt us. In those cases, don't waste time and energy waiting for something that may never happen. Instead, take the opportunity to forgive and move forward.

As covered earlier, forgiveness doesn't imply weakness so let go and turn the page to your next chapter. Doing so will open up many new doors of hope and opportunity for you. Choose to be empowered by this new season, and seek God's direction as you enter it.

Forgiveness does not always mean reconciling with the person who hurt you. It's possible to forgive someone and still choose to not have that person in your life. As previously discussed, forgiveness doesn't imply that you endorse or accept the behavior that led to the pain or deception. It means letting go of the negative emotions toward the person who caused it. Forgiveness is a process and it takes time. It's normal for feelings of anger, hurt, and resentment to resurface, and it's important to continue to work through them. As covered earlier, forgiveness doesn't imply weakness. It takes a great deal of strength and courage to forgive someone who has hurt you.

The Bible is filled with wisdom and guidance that can help us work through difficult times of transition. Ecclesiastes 3:1–8 (NIV) is a great passage to remember when you're struggling to find closure and are ready to move forward without it. The scripture reminds us that "there is a time for everything, and a season for every activity under the heavens." This passage also encourages us to "seek peace and pursue it," even when we don't have all the answers. It also reminds us that there is a natural ebb and flow to life. Sometimes we experience joy; sometimes we experience sorrow. Sometimes we must let go of things or people that are no longer serving us, and sometimes we must hold on to them. Sometimes we need to speak up and take action, and other times we need to be quiet and listen. There may be a time to forgive someone who has hurt us and a time to let go of that hurt and move forward with our lives. Similarly, there may be a time to seek closure on a particular chapter of our lives and a time to embrace a new beginning.

It is difficult to move forward without forgiving those who have hurt us, and while it isn't always easy to get past grudges and resentments, it is essential for our own growth. We must remember that "love covers a multitude of sins" (1 Peter 4:8 ESV) and that the power of God can help us forgive even when we don't feel like we are able to.

The Bible reminds us that "God is our refuge and strength, a very present help in trouble." (Psalm 46:1). When it feels like we can't go on without closure, we can find strength, comfort, and purpose in Him. He will lead us through this difficult season and help us to embrace our next chapter with courage and faith. Don't wait for closure, but instead, open your heart to God and allow Him to work in you so that you can move forward without it. He will provide the peace and hope that are essential for growth.

And we know that all things work together for good to them that love God, to them who are the called according to His purpose (Romans 8:28 NKJV). The things that God does in our lives and the incidents and situations that happen in many instances will make you feel that He doesn't care. There is a reason for the riddle. There is an answer to the question, clarity to the confusion, and calmness in the chaos. There is a time and purpose to everything under the sun. God will work all things together for good if we put our trust in Him. If we learn how to forgive, He will give us closure and release healing. No matter what situation you face, don't wait for closure from others. Embrace your next chapter, and move forward with forgiveness. This is what the Bible tells us to do.

> The Bible also reminds us in Isaiah 43:19 (KJV):
> "Behold, I will do a new thing,
> Now it shall spring forth;
> Shall you not know it?
> I will even make a road in the wilderness
> And rivers in the desert."

This message reminds us that God is constantly working in our lives, even when we can't perceive or comprehend it. We should trust in His plans and embrace the new opportunities He brings into our lives. This is a promise of God's faithfulness.

Life is a journey full of twists and turns. It's a story that has no definite end. But instead of getting fixated on closure, why not embrace your next chapter and move forward? Don't wait for things to be perfect or for everything to fall into place before you start pursuing your dreams. Life is unpredictable, and waiting for closure may only lead to missed opportunities. Sometimes the best way to find closure is by starting a new chapter in life. It takes courage to step out of your comfort zone, but it's worth it. So, leave the past behind, embrace your present, and start building a new and fulfilling future. Remember, every chapter of your life is an opportunity to create a masterpiece.

Reflection Questions

1. What do I need to forgive myself for so that I can move forward?

2. How have past mistakes prevented me from embracing my next chapter?

3. What does forgiveness mean to me, and why is it important for healing?

4. How do I let go of the hurt and disappointment that hold me back?

5. How can I show compassion for those who have aggrieved, offended, or hurt me and still move forward with my life?

6. What are some practical steps that I can take to help me embrace a new chapter in my life?

TRUSTING GOD IN
the Process *of*
Forgiveness

"I can do all things through Christ who
strengthens me." Philippians 4:13 (NKJV)

This chapter explores the challenges of forgiveness when we have experienced deep pain and hurt. It acknowledges that forgiveness can feel impossible in certain situations but emphasizes the importance of working toward forgiveness for our own well-being and healing. Ultimately, the chapter encourages readers to continue the work of forgiveness even in the face of pain and difficulty, recognizing that forgiveness is a journey that requires ongoing effort and commitment.

Society has been conditioned to seek justice and pursue reconciliation. We read countless stories of how people have been victims of senseless acts. Throughout history, forgiveness has been a continuing struggle. The struggle with forgiveness happens when a person experiences an injustice or violation that causes deep emotional or physical pain. Emotional or physical pain, which is the same as hurt, translates into feelings of frustration and loss. Hurt in most produces anger and an uncontrollable drive for revenge in some form, which oftentimes leads to vindictiveness and unfocused hostility. Also, people who struggle to forgive nurture their anger to pay back the offenders with greater pain and intensity. They become rigid in other relationships, suffer from trust issues, and develop a pattern of not giving unless they receive something in return with a weird sense of competitiveness that should never exist in relationships.

Some situations are so emotionally charged that seeking forgiveness can lead to more hurt rather than healing. Forgiveness requires the offender to accept responsibility for their actions, which may be too painful for them or the victim. Furthermore, in many cases, an apology or display of remorse may not be enough to repair the harm done and only serve to deepen the rift between two people. When reconciliation is not possible, it is important to focus on self-care and acceptance rather than forcing a resolution that may ultimately be more damaging. In these cases, it is important to remember that forgiveness does not have to be associated with reconciliation or restoration of a relationship; instead, it can mean allowing oneself to let go of bitterness and resentment while still maintaining healthy boundaries. This can allow both the victim and the offender to move forward in a healthier, more positive way. Ultimately, forgiveness is a deeply personal process that should be undertaken when both parties are ready and willing to engage with it in a meaningful way. If reconciliation or restoration is not possible, focusing on self-care and acceptance can be an important part of the healing process.

No matter what form it takes, forgiveness is a powerful tool that has the potential to bring peace and resolution in even the most difficult of situations. By allowing ourselves to recognize our own hurt and pain without letting it define us, we can open the door to making peace with our pasts. We all at one time or another have said, "I should forgive, but…" and so start to develop deep wounds of anger and bitterness that never seem to heal because forgiveness is not enough.

It is difficult to give up negative feelings that have been brought on by some act of injustice from someone. Don't I have a right to feel hurt? After all, I was violated. It doesn't make much sense. In essence, you may be reading this now and saying to yourself, "I've experienced hurt, and as a result, I have very real feelings of anger, bitterness, and even resentment depending on the level of offense." Matthew 24:10 (NKJV) says, "And then shall many be offended, and shall betray one another, and shall hate one another." How do we escape the issue of forgiveness? Why do we need to forgive? Should I reserve the right to hold someone accountable when they hurt me? These are questions that constantly surface as the topic of forgiveness is explored.

Matthew 6:14–15 (KJV) says, "For if ye forgive men their trespasses, your heavenly Father will also forgive you: But if ye forgive not men their trespasses, neither will your

Father forgive your trespasses." In other words, for God to forgive your sins, you must first forgive those who have offended you. What about those who have been victimized without any provocation? What about the victims of terrorism and other crimes? Can we forget about the innocent victims due to molestation and rape?

Forgiveness extends beyond feeling. It takes into account what happened and your emotional response and feelings in the moment. It is a conscious choice to release the pain, hurt, and anger associated with an event and accept that it happened. When we forgive, we can start to move on from our suffering, opening a space where peace can settle in our hearts. As we've discussed before, the process of forgiving isn't about erasing memories or approving someone's wrongdoings. Instead, it involves acknowledging and accepting the reality of what has happened. This practice can free up your energy, allowing you to connect with yourself in a deeper, more meaningful way. Forgiveness can be an ongoing process, as it can take time to truly heal from the hurt that's been caused. But by giving yourself permission to forgive and being mindful of your own needs, you will begin to notice a shift in how you feel. The act of forgiveness is ultimately about self-care, helping us to reconnect with our inner peace and allowing us to move through life with grace. It's a powerful reminder that no matter what has happened, we can choose to make space for healing and growth.

We do not prepare for major issues that come and tear us apart inside. It may seem easier to forgive what is done to us, per se, than the violation of a loved one. Hurt after it is conceived, in most, produces anger and an uncontrollable drive for revenge in some form, which oftentimes leads to vindictiveness and unfocused hostility. Sometimes, just observing the offender receive what is in our minds "just recompense" seems gratifying and justifying.

The parents of a young girl who was the victim of a tragic hit-and-run shared their story, stating that the offender pleaded guilty to DUI-invoked manslaughter charges. The car carrying the mother, sister, and young girl was rear-ended resulting in the tragic loss of the young girl and critical injuries to the eighteen-year-old sister. The offender's blood alcohol level exceeded the legal limit. Throughout the trial, remorse and regret filled the room. While addressing the family, the offender apologized profusely and stated that he never meant to hurt the family as he had been hurt.

Why wouldn't this mother be justified in not granting pardon or harboring feelings of resentment? An apology cannot undo the hurt that has been caused or the anguish that will be experienced. How could those affected by the death of this innocent child ever forget this horrific incident? Forgiving and forgetting would be almost like giving him a pass or even worse, letting him off the hook.

Making this choice is challenging for anyone, and I don't have a definitive answer. However, what I can assure you is that forgiving doesn't equate to endorsing the act or surrendering our claim to justice. It means that we are willing to move forward from this tragedy in order to bring peace and healing into our own lives. It's not easy, and it takes courage to choose compassion and grace over resentment and hate. But if we can find a way to forgive, then we can begin the process of healing.

As discussed before, we must learn to forgive those who have hurt us, not because we condone their actions, but because it's the only way to move forward and free ourselves of that hurt. Forgiveness is the key to unlocking our true potential and finding peace within ourselves.

To begin the process of forgiveness, it's important to recognize that individuals have the autonomy to make their own choices, and our own reactions are solely our responsibility. If we hold on to anger and bitterness, it will ultimately result in more suffering. Forgiveness is a spiritual practice that enables us to release ourselves from negative feelings and grants us the opportunity to discover inner peace.

In this sad situation, it may not be easy to forgive, but finding a way to do so will ultimately help the family move forward and heal. If you are dealing with your own set of unique circumstances, whether it's through prayer, counseling, or simply opening up a conversation—take the courageous steps of forgiveness and free yourselves from suffering.

No matter how dark and lonely the moment may seem, we must put our trust in God and find a way to forgive. As hard as it may be, by forgiving those who have aggrieved, offended, or hurt us, we open ourselves up to His grace and mercy. We can take comfort in knowing that God's love and compassion will never leave us.

We must remember that we are all human; no one is perfect, and we have all made mistakes. Although forgiveness may take time, it is only through forgiveness that we can truly heal and begin to move forward with our lives.

A few years ago, a woman disclosed during a Christian counseling session that she entered into a new relationship with a man after going through an abusive marriage of eighteen years and a bitter divorce. Her new relationship started wonderfully, as most relationships do in the beginning stages. Everything was blissful and amazing. One evening they planned to have dinner, but he stated that he was not feeling well and would not be able to join her. She decided to stop by his house to check in on him after numerous unsuccessful attempts to contact him. She noticed that there were no signs of anyone at his home and grew even more concerned. She remembered that she had access to his voice mails and decided to listen. She noticed that a couple of women had left messages suggesting that they were planning to connect at some point during the evening. She decided to wait to confront him when he arrived home. After confronting him regarding the issue, she found out that he had been with five other women, so they decided to end the relationship. A month after the relationship ended, she started developing headaches and other symptoms similar to the flu, so she scheduled a visit to the doctor. Her test results came back positive for HIV.

Although we don't know the details of the relationship, we could agree that the outcome was more of a punishment than anything else. This woman left an abusive relationship to end up suffering another form of abuse. The lies, the cheating, and the deceit all led to the end of a relationship while contracting a disease. Although this does not mark the end of life for her, she will need to be extremely careful to ensure that she does not repeat this cycle. How can she ever find forgiveness?

She was finally able to take the time to heal. She learned to forgive herself first before she was able to move on and forgive her former partner. Forgiveness does not mean that you are giving the person a pass for their actions, it simply means that you are releasing your negative energy associated with the experience. It might be helpful to find a support system and engage in activities that promote healing and renewal. She began writing down her thoughts, exploring meditation, engaging with friends and family, and even seeking out a faith-based direction to bring her peace. Taking time to reflect on the experience allowed this woman to gain strength and learn from the situation so she can make better decisions in the future. It was important for her to realize her purpose and future, regardless of what happened.

In 2004, a woman was married to her husband of five years with a plan to have children. On the outside, things seemed to be well in the marriage. He was well established in his career, their ministry was thriving, and she had a home-based business, living in an affluent community. She was a faithful, loving wife, and everything seemed perfect until the day she found out that he had been with several other women. The larger issue is that he left her with an STD as a result of his infidelity. The STD created internal scarring and damage to her reproductive organs, ultimately leading to infertility. She was broken, and so many thoughts raced through her mind. What had she done to deserve this? So many unanswered questions.

This unfortunate woman was left not only bearing emotional wounds but suffered permanent physical damage as a result of her ex-husband's reckless behavior and extramarital affairs. It was a devastating blow, but she held on to faith in God and determined that both her infertility and unsuccessful marriage due to infidelity wouldn't stop her. She would not allow bitterness and unforgiveness to paralyze her. She chose to focus on her faith and trust that God had a plan for her life.

She committed to using everything she had been through as an opportunity for growth and developed a passion for helping other women who were going through infertility issues due to infidelity or other circumstances. She became an advocate, speaking out about the struggles of infertility and facing reproductive challenges.

Her inspiring story encourages other women to keep fighting no matter their circumstances and to stay committed to finding the hope, faith, and strength that can come from adversity. Her story is a reminder that no matter what life throws at us, we have the power to overcome. She has gone from being a victim of circumstance to becoming an advocate for change and living out her life's purpose in a way that is truly inspiring. Her journey to success is a living example of the power of resilience and determination.

Several years ago, a mother pleaded for the retaliation to cease and an opportunity to forgive those who had murdered her eldest son. Even with tears in her eyes, she sought after God for consolation and guidance during this time of grieving and the strength needed to deal with the pain of her loss. She pursued every possible way to avoid revenge on the offenders and maintained her faith in God. Although she feared for her own life, the cycle of grief set in, causing her emotions to spiral out of control as she vacillated between the choice to deny or accept what she was feeling, to forgive or not.

Yet she stayed firm in her faith, believing that God had a plan. Through her prayers and devotion to God, the mother found solace and comfort in the knowledge that her son was now at peace. As a reminder of his love for us, she accepted the tragedy as an opportunity to grow closer to God. She determined not to allow her pain and sorrow to rule her life so that she could be an example of hope and faith in the midst of adversity.

In times of distress, we may feel helpless and vulnerable, as if there is no escape from our current situation. But this mother's story serves as a reminder that no matter how dark things seem, there is always a way out. Through prayer and trust in God, we can persevere through our suffering and find peace of mind. So take courage and have faith that God will bring you comfort and solace when it seems like all hope is lost. And remember: with every hardship comes an opportunity to grow closer to God and live life to the fullest. He will never leave you alone.

When we feel aggrieved, offended, or hurt, it's natural to want justice and retaliation. Retaliation can give us a sense of satisfaction, but if our actions are driven by anger or bitterness, it can cause more harm and suffering for everyone involved.

Retaliation is responding to an action with another action that is intended to harm or punish the person who committed the original action. It is a form of revenge, and it can take many forms such as physical violence, verbal abuse, spreading rumors or gossip, or seeking to ruin someone's reputation.

Retaliation is often motivated by feelings of anger, hurt, or injustice, and it can be seen as an attempt to assert control over a situation or to restore a sense of balance or fairness. However, retaliation can be harmful and can lead to further conflicts, negative consequences, and escalation of violence. Retaliation is different from forgiveness, as forgiveness is about letting go of negative emotions and choosing to not respond in a harmful way. It's about moving forward and working toward a better future. Retaliation, on the other hand, is about seeking to hurt or harm the person who caused the hurt or betrayal.

The Bible teaches us that vengeance is the Lord's, and we should leave it to Him. Instead of retaliating against those who hurt us, we should pray for them and ask God to bring justice and healing into their lives. As believers in Christ, we can trust that He will take care of our enemies if we turn to Him.

The Bible also commands us to love our enemies, even when they hurt us. By loving our enemies, we are showing them the same mercy and grace that Jesus showed us when He died on the cross for our sins. We can do this by praying for those who hurt us, forgiving them, and showing compassion in place of anger or bitterness.

Retaliating against those who hurt us does not bring healing or peace but instead can cause greater pain and suffering.

Resentment is an emotional state of holding a grudge, harboring ill will, or bitterness toward someone for something they have done or failed to do. Resentment may arise toward an individual, a group, or a circumstance that resulted in pain or deceit. It is an emotional state of feeling offended, mistreated, or unappreciated. Resentment can also come as a result of being slighted, disrespected, or disregarded. Examples of that would be feeling unappreciated for your efforts, being taken advantage of, or not receiving recognition or credit for something you did.

Other examples of that would be feeling ignored or neglected, being treated unfairly, feeling like you are not valued, feeling like your opinion doesn't matter, or someone making you feel inferior in comparison to another. Betrayal, jealousy, and envy can also lead to resentment. Examples of this would be feeling betrayed by a friend or loved one, feeling overlooked or taken for granted in relationships, and experiencing envy because of someone else's success or achievements. Other examples include feeling jealous when someone else is given attention or recognition instead of you or feeling taken advantage of when you are expected to contribute or give more than what is expected. Persistent negative interactions can also cause feelings of resentment. If someone constantly points out your deficiencies or mistakes, constantly makes fun of you or certain attributes about you, belittles you by name-calling, or constantly displays negative behaviors, you may start to feel resentful of that person. Resentment and retaliation are two sides of the same coin. It's important to recognize when resentment is taking root in our hearts, as it can lead to thoughts of revenge or retaliation.

Vindictiveness can also manifest as a desire to see the person who hurt you suffer in some way. This can include wanting them to experience the same pain they caused you or wanting them to experience negative consequences as a result of their actions. Some examples of vindictiveness include wanting the person to be punished, wanting them to feel embarrassed or ashamed, wanting them to struggle and suffer, and wishing they will experience hurt or pain similar to what they caused you. Other examples are seeking revenge, wanting to destroy the person's reputation or relationships, and wanting them to be punished in a court of law. Make no mistake, justice should be served if a law is broken. However, oftentimes our desire for justice can become a form of vindictiveness that is born out of the need for revenge.

Resentment and vindictiveness are both incredibly destructive emotions that can lead to serious psychological damage. Instead, choose to forgive and free yourself. Forgiveness is a powerful tool that can help us heal, restore relationships, and create a brighter future for ourselves and those around us. When we choose to forgive instead of retaliate or seek revenge, it frees us from the burden of anger, hurt, and bitterness. It also allows us to experience a sense of peace, hope, and joy that comes from knowing we are not defined by our past traumas or setbacks.

God's love is powerful enough to help us overcome even the most difficult emotions and experiences. He wants us to be free from the pain of vengeance and resentment so that we can live in harmony with ourselves and those around us. So remember that in the face of adversity, God is always with you and willing to forgive. No matter what hurt or betrayal you have experienced, let go of the resentment and choose to find peace through forgiveness and faith in Him.

Forgiveness is a process that isn't always easy. It can be a long and arduous journey, filled with many ups and downs. But through it all, we must remember to trust in God. He is the ultimate guide in the journey toward forgiveness. Without His direction, we may stumble and falter, but with His help, we can achieve true forgiveness. It's important to remember that forgiveness is a choice, not a feeling. By choosing to forgive, we allow ourselves to break free from the chains of resentment and bitterness. It may take time, but when we choose to trust in God and follow His lead, the process of forgiveness can be not only achievable but incredibly rewarding.

It is not easy to trust when we have been hurt by those we love. But it is essential that we trust God's plan for our lives if we are to move forward and find peace within ourselves. Believing in God and trusting Him during the process of forgiveness is important with us having faith in His perfect plan for our lives, even if it deviates from our original expectations. In Jeremiah 29:11 (KJV), the Scriptures state, "For I know the thoughts that I think toward you, saith the Lord, thoughts of peace, and not of evil, to give you an expected end." God's plan is bigger than anything you could ever face. His plan is greater than any situation or issue that exists.

When we are faced with uncertainty and confusion, it can be difficult to trust in God's plan. But it is crucial that we do so, even when we don't fully understand it. So how do we cultivate this trust? We must seek God's wisdom, pray for clarity and understanding, and align our hearts with His desires. With time and patience, we will begin to see the bigger picture and understand that God always knows what is best for us. Even in our most painful experiences, we can take heart in the fact that God has the power to turn them into something good. We may not see the blessings at the moment, but over time, we will recognize them. Through it all, we must remember that God's grace is sufficient for us. It is only through Him that we can find the strength to endure and the hope to carry on. So let us trust in His plan and take comfort in the knowledge that He is always with us, guiding us every step of the way.

Reflection Questions

1. What are some situations or people in my life that I struggle to forgive? How has this impacted my emotional well-being?

2. What is my current understanding of forgiveness, and how does it align with the author's perspective in forgiving beyond my own pain?

3. What are some specific strategies or practices suggested by the author that resonate with me, and how can I incorporate them into my own life and journey of healing?

4. How can I use my own experiences of forgiveness and healing to empathize with and support others who may be struggling with similar challenges?

5. How can I move forward in my own journey of forgiveness and healing with compassion and grace, both for myself and for those who have hurt me?

FORGIVENESS IS NOT WEAKNESS:
ACKNOWLEDGING OUR
STRENGTH *by*
SETTING BOUNDARIES

"And not only that, but we also rejoice in our afflictions, because we know that affliction produces endurance, endurance produces proven character, and proven character produces hope." Romans 5:3–4 (HSCB)

In this chapter, we will look at the importance of boundaries in order to protect our emotional health. We'll explore different techniques for setting healthy limits and respecting others' boundaries. Additionally, we will discuss how to hold ourselves accountable and create a safe space for healing.

When it comes to our emotional health, boundaries can be a powerful tool. Having healthy boundaries helps us protect ourselves from being taken advantage of and set expectations for how we want to be treated. Boundaries are also important for creating a safe space for healing, where we can let go of any pain and stress we may have been carrying around.

It is important to remember that forgiveness doesn't mean you are weak; it actually reveals your strength and determination. We must learn how to forgive those who have hurt, aggrieved, or offended us, while also setting boundaries to protect ourselves from being hurt again. It can be difficult to forgive someone who has hurt or betrayed you, and it can be even harder to set boundaries with them. When setting boundaries, know that you have the right to protect your mental, emotional, and physical well-being.

Sometimes we are wounded as a result of the trust that we have given to another person. We may not always know exactly what our boundaries are when we first start out in a relationship. However, as we learn more about ourselves and what we are comfortable with, it is important to communicate our boundaries with those around us. Communication is also key here, as it is important to explain our boundaries to those we let into our lives.

As we learn more about ourselves and what is best for us, we can create healthier boundaries that help us feel safe and secure. Creating healthy boundaries also enables us to express ourselves authentically without fear of judgment or manipulation because those boundaries are just as important to the other person as they are to you.

Having healthy boundaries is a practice of self-love and respect, allowing us to nurture our emotional health and well-being. When we are mindful of our own boundaries, we are better able to create mutually respectful relationships with those around us. By establishing healthy boundaries, we can also be more present in the moment and connect with ourselves more deeply.

Our emotional health is an important part of our overall well-being, and setting healthy boundaries is one way to help us nurture this aspect of ourselves. We all deserve to be heard, respected, and loved. By creating safe spaces for ourselves through boundaries, we can take the first step toward real transformation.

When it comes to emotional health, it's essential that we take the time to set healthy boundaries for ourselves so that we can protect our hearts and minds from hurtful and damaging experiences. Setting boundaries also allows us to have healthy relationships with those around us, so we can engage in meaningful conversations and exchanges of love, support, and understanding. It can be quite refreshing as you are establishing emotional boundaries and respecting the boundaries of others. When we come from a place of respect for ourselves and others, it helps create an atmosphere of understanding and trust that can be incredibly healing for us.

Setting healthy boundaries can be a difficult process, as it requires us to be honest with ourselves and those around us. We must take the time to identify what we are comfortable with and what we are not comfortable with and communicate those expectations clearly. It is also important to talk to our partners, family members, and friends about the boundaries that we have set so that they can respect them.

In order to hold ourselves accountable, we must take the time to reflect on whether our boundaries are being respected or violated. If we feel like our limits are not being respected, it is important that we address this with those involved and make any necessary adjustments.

Creating healthy boundaries can help us foster self-love and respect as well as open up a space for healing. By learning how to set limits and stick to them, we can create an atmosphere of trust and safety that will allow us to move through our emotional health struggles with grace and understanding. With these tools in hand, we can make sure that our emotional health is being taken care of and that we are honoring ourselves in the process.

It's easy to mistake boundaries as a way to shut people out, but in reality, they serve a much greater purpose. Boundaries are about creating healthy relationships with the people around us. Setting boundaries isn't just about saying no or creating distance. It's about taking care of ourselves and others in a way that fosters respect, trust, and understanding. It's about being honest and upfront about our needs and wants while also being open and receptive to the needs and wants of those we care about.

This can be especially beneficial when it comes to forgiveness, as it allows us to forgive without completely letting go of our pain or allowing someone else's actions to define us. By creating boundaries around our own emotions, we can more easily practice self-compassion and recognize that though something may have hurt us, it does not have to be our entire story. We can draw a line between our own feelings and those of the other person and recognize that while someone may have hurt, aggrieved, or offended us, they do not control how we choose to respond. By creating boundaries and affirming our right to be respected and safe, we can more easily remove the sting from the event and forgive without relinquishing our own emotions or sense of self. Doing this allows us to reclaim our power and move forward with grace, strength, and understanding. Through creating boundaries in the process of forgiveness, we can finally let go of any resentment or pain that we may have carried for far too long. Boundaries enable us to recognize our own feelings while still recognizing that those feelings are separate from the other person, allowing us to forgive and move on from past hurts in a more healthy and balanced way.

Additionally, it helps us to realize that it is possible to forgive without forgetting or condoning someone else's actions. By acknowledging our own pain, we can make space for forgiveness without letting someone else's actions define us or continue to hurt us. Creating boundaries in our process of forgiveness helps us to open up to peace and acceptance while still protecting our hearts and minds from further harm.

Proverbs 4:23 (NIV), says, "Above all else, guard your heart, for everything you do flows from it." This verse emphasizes the importance of protecting one's heart from negative influences such as anger, bitterness, and resentment. This is important because these negative feelings can prevent us from properly forgiving others. Our emotions can be deceiving when we are hurt, misused, or done wrong. What's worse is that if you decide to forgive, others will either make you feel like that was a bad decision or make you feel guilty for choosing to do what is right. Others will make disparaging comments and negative remarks about you. An old adage says, "Meekness is often mistaken for weakness." This could not be further from the truth. It takes a strong person to forgive! When you choose to forgive rather than hold on to bitterness and anger, it is a sign of strength—an act of courage that demonstrates your ability to rise above the situation. You can set boundaries that will help protect against future offenses while still choosing grace and mercy.

The verse speaks volumes about the significance of wisdom and discernment in our relationships with others. It cautions us to be mindful of who we allow into our lives and to set clear boundaries in order to safeguard both ourselves and our relationships. It is a lighthouse that beams a light on the path toward healthier and more fulfilling connections.

We should forgive others not because of what they do, but because God commands us to show grace and mercy to them. It is not contingent on whether they ask to be forgiven. Although forgiveness is important, it's important to note that it doesn't always mean that it's safe or healthy to rebuild a relationship to its previous state, especially if the person who caused harm hasn't shown genuine remorse or is unwilling to change their behavior. Proverbs 22:24–25 (RSV) says, "Make no friendship with a man given to anger, nor go with a wrathful man, lest you learn his ways and entangle yourself in a snare." This is a call for us to be intentional and discerning about the people we allow in our lives and with whom we choose to associate ourselves with. When there is a conflict or disagreement, not apologizing can indicate anger or pride. This behavior can harm relationships. Avoiding responsibility and an apology can result in bitterness, resentment, and negative patterns of behavior involving others.

When it comes to the people we surround ourselves with, it's crucial that we select those who possess qualities like humility, honesty, and a desire to work through conflicts. By doing so, we begin to cultivate the kind of relationships that help us establish healthy boundaries.

Don't underestimate the power of your inner circle. Who we choose to associate with can shape our values, beliefs, and actions in profound ways. Seek out those who inspire you, who challenge you to be better, who lift you up when you need it most, and who will appreciate your presence. Remember, you have a choice. Surround yourself with the kind of people who push you to be your best self, and watch as your life begins to transform before your very eyes. This is how we began to establish boundaries.

Colossians 3:13 (NIV), says, "Bear with each other and forgive one another if any of you has a grievance against someone. Forgive as the Lord forgave you." This verse encourages forgiveness as an act of grace and reminds us that we are called to forgive as we have been forgiven by God. This verse highlights the importance of forgiveness in maintaining healthy relationships but also acknowledges that it may be necessary to bear with one another and set appropriate boundaries in order to promote healing and reconciliation.

However, the verse does suggest that it may be necessary to "bear with each other," which could imply setting boundaries to protect oneself or others from harm. For example, if someone has a pattern of behavior that is harmful or abusive, it may be necessary to set limits on one's interactions with them, in order to protect oneself or others from further harm.

In addition, the verse emphasizes the importance of forgiveness, which is a key aspect of setting boundaries in healthy relationships. Forgiveness does not require forgetting or excusing harmful behavior. Rather, it involves releasing anger and resentment and choosing to show compassion and grace toward others. This can assist in fostering healing and reconciliation in relationships while also establishing boundaries to ensure the safety of oneself and others.

Forgiveness is an act of strength, not weakness. Acknowledging our own worth and setting boundaries are crucial in order to practice forgiveness. It takes courage and a deep sense of self-love to forgive those who have wronged us, but it also requires a clear understanding that our boundaries must be respected. It is important to remember that forgiveness does not mean forgetting or excusing the harm that has been done, but rather choosing to let go of the anger and resentment that may be holding us back from growth and healing. By setting healthy boundaries, we show ourselves the respect and love we deserve while also creating a space for healing and connection with those we have forgiven. Let us embrace forgiveness as a powerful and transformative force that allows us to move forward with grace and resilience.

Reflection Questions

1. What are some situations in which I struggle to set and maintain healthy boundaries?

2. How can I differentiate between healthy boundaries and walls that prevent me from connecting with others?

3. How have past experiences with boundary violations impacted my emotional well-being and relationships?

4. How can I communicate my boundaries effectively and assertively while maintaining respect and empathy for others?

5. What practices can I incorporate into my daily routine to help me prioritize and maintain healthy boundaries?

LIVING IN FREEDOM: THE MIRACLE *of* TRUE FORGIVENESS

"Remember not the former things, nor consider the things of old. Behold, I am doing a new thing; now it springs forth, do you not perceive it? I will make a way in the wilderness and rivers in the desert."

Isaiah 43:18–19 (ESV)

This chapter of the book provides an inspiring look into the power of forgiveness and how living with a forgiving heart can unlock true freedom from pain, suffering, hurt, and resentment. It references Isaiah 43:18–19 to remind us that God is always at work to bring new life and hope out of our struggles. As we learn to forgive, let go of the past, and move forward with confidence, may we continually trust that God is with us every step of the way.

Forgiveness can be one of the most difficult things to do, both emotionally and mentally. There are many factors that make it difficult, from fear of vulnerability and trust to feeling as if you are betraying yourself by forgiving someone who has hurt, aggrieved, or offended you. It can be difficult to forgive because it can take a lot of courage and strength. It's often easier to remain angry and not forgive than it is to let go and move forward.

Forgiveness can be emotionally draining because of the many emotions that come with it. You may experience intense anger, sadness, guilt, fear, or shame. These emotions can be hard to manage as they can be deeply embedded in the mind. It can be difficult to let go of these feelings and move on, as they are often part of our identity.

Whenever we find it hard to forgive, it can be a challenging and emotionally taxing process. We feel stuck in our hurt and anger and can struggle to move forward. But ultimately, forgiving is important for our emotional well-being as well as for the rebuilding of relationships. The process of healing from past hurts and moving forward can be a long journey, but it is possible.

The process of healing involves understanding and accepting our feelings, learning from them, and allowing ourselves to grow as individuals. This growth is integral to the healing process; it helps us become more self-aware, strong, and resilient. When we understand how our emotions influence us and make changes based on this knowledge, we can start to heal.

Reiterating our previous points, remember that forgiveness is not a mark of weakness or giving in. Rather, it is an act of strength and courage which enables us to accept our own emotions, while creating space for understanding and compassion toward others. When we move through the pain and hurt with grace, self-compassion, and forgiveness, we can start to heal.

It is also important to understand that it takes time for emotional wounds to heal. Depending on the situation, the healing process may take months or even years. It is a journey—one that requires patience and self-reflection. While there may be setbacks along the way, it is important to remain open and honest with oneself while focusing on self-care.

The Bible teaches that forgiveness is essential to living in freedom and experiencing the miracle of true forgiveness. Something amazing happens when we choose to forgive others that impacts our mental, physical, emotional, and spiritual sides. It can reduce stress and anxiety levels by releasing negative emotions and reducing the burden of grudges and resentments. It can improve our relationships by reducing conflict and improving communication and trust. It can increase our ability to empathize with others and demonstrate compassion, leading to greater emotional intelligence and quality relationships. It can enhance our self-esteem by helping us to feel more empowered and in control of our emotions and reactions. Studies have shown an improvement in physical health outcomes, such as lower blood pressure, reduced inflammation, and improved immune function.

Mentally, we free ourselves from the internal bondage of bitterness and resentment. Physically, our minds and bodies are transformed as tension is released. Tension creates physical pain, and when it is released, the body experiences a newfound freedom. On an emotional level, we experience inner peace as we free ourselves from the grip of anger, bitterness, and rage, releasing any grudges against others. Emotional freedom is essential for true joy and peace.

Jesus said, "For if you forgive others their trespasses, your heavenly Father will also forgive you" (Matthew 6:14 ESV). When we choose to forgive, our spiritual relationship with God is strengthened and deepened as we align ourselves more closely with His will and character. We are liberated from the bondage of our past hurts that have weighed us down for so long. Our connection to God's love is strengthened and our faith grows more deeply rooted in His will for us, and we open doors to receive blessings that have been hindered by unforgiveness.

Forgiveness is the key to true freedom, and it starts with us. As we forgive, we can experience a miracle that changes our lives in ways we never imagined. When we offer forgiveness to those who have hurt us, God begins to work his miracles in our midst. He frees us from our pain and provides us with a new perspective on life.

In fact, Jesus himself emphasized the importance of forgiveness, teaching his disciples to pray: "forgive us our debts, as we also have forgiven our debtors" (Matthew 6:12 KJV). He also told the parable of the unmerciful servant, who was forgiven a great debt by his master but then refused to forgive a small debt owed to him by another servant. Jesus emphasized that we must forgive others from our hearts, just as God has forgiven us (Matthew 18:21–35). We are commanded to apply grace and mercy to others just as it has been freely given to us.

Living with a forgiving heart is not always easy, but it is essential to experiencing the fullness of God's grace and freedom. Jesus said, "Blessed are the merciful, for they shall receive mercy" (Matthew 5:7 KJV). This means that if we are willing to forgive, we will receive mercy in return. It is a miraculous cycle of grace that brings fullness and joy into our lives.

As human beings, we have the capacity to hold on to anger, bitterness, and resentment. But what if we choose to let go of those negative emotions and instead offer grace and compassion to others, even in circumstances where they don't seem worthy of it? What would society look like if we all chose to forgive even when it is hard to do? We can create a culture of forgiveness and compassion, one that allows us to move on to greater things with God. We must remember that our capacity for forgiving others comes from our experience of being forgiven by God. As He has given us mercy, so too should we extend it to those around us. We are called to forgive, just as we have been forgiven.

It is not always easy to forgive those who have wronged us, but in doing so, we can experience the true power of grace and mercy. When we choose to offer forgiveness, we break down barriers between ourselves and God and open our hearts up to His healing love. Forgiveness is a gift we can give to ourselves and others; it is an act of courage that brings us closer to God and allows us to experience the fullness of His grace.

Forgiveness is a powerful choice that requires both strength and humility. It means acknowledging when we have wronged others and seeking their forgiveness. At the same time, it means extending forgiveness to those who have hurt us, even when we may not feel they deserve it.

Forgiveness may be difficult, but it is worth the effort. As we choose to forgive, we open ourselves up to God's healing grace and peace. We come closer to understanding the power of His mercy and how He can use us to bring about reconciliation and hope in a broken world.

To reemphasize our previous point, remember that to offer forgiveness is not synonymous with weakness, but of strength. It shows that we trust in God's power to bring healing and hope, even when it may seem impossible. Choosing to forgive is not an easy path, but it is one that can bring profound healing and growth. When we let go of our anger and choose to extend grace instead, we open ourselves up to new possibilities and deeper connections with others. So let us choose forgiveness, not just for the sake of others but for our own sake as well.

Living with a forgiving heart not only sets us free from the burden of unforgiveness, but it also aligns us with the character of Christ, who forgave those who crucified him. By following His example, we can witness the transformative power of forgiveness in our own lives and relationships. Don't hold on to grudges. Embrace forgiveness, and let it bring you freedom, joy, and transformation.

Freedom is a concept that we all strive for, yet it can be difficult to achieve without true forgiveness. Forgiveness is, in essence, the key that unlocks the door to freedom. It allows us to let go of the past and move forward without the weight of resentment and bitterness holding us back. It is truly miraculous in its ability to help us release the pain and hurt that we carry and instead focus on the present moment. When we forgive, we begin to see the world through a new lens, one that is filled with hope, love, and infinite possibilities. It may not always be easy, but at the end of the day, the freedom that comes with true forgiveness is well worth the effort. So take the first step on this journey toward a life of freedom, and embrace the miracle of true forgiveness.

Reflection Questions

1. What specific steps can I take to prioritize my emotional healing and growth in my daily life?

2. How can I use my past experiences as a source of strength and resilience rather than allowing them to hold me back?

3. What role does self-care play in my emotional healing process, and how can I incorporate more self-care practices into my daily routine?

4. How can I use my newfound awareness and self-reflection to create positive change in my relationships and interactions with others?

5. How can I remain open and curious about my own emotional healing process and continue to learn and grow over time?

CELEBRATING THE LIBERATION *of* FORGIVENESS IN OUR LIVES

*"He will again have compassion on us; he will tread our
iniquities underfoot. You will cast all our sins into the
depths of the sea. You will show faithfulness to Jacob and
love to Abraham, as he has sworn to our fathers
from days of old." Micah 7:19–20 (ESV)*

In this chapter, we will conclude by looking at all that we
have explored in this book. We'll review the different
steps of healing from emotional wounds and discuss how to
use these tools to create a life full of joy and emotional
freedom. Additionally, we will offer some words of
encouragement on our spiritual journey to finding peace and
well-being. The journey of forgiveness is a lifelong process
that requires deep commitment and courage. As we learn to
forgive others and ourselves, we are liberated from the pain

of the past, open to new possibilities in the present, and set on a course for healing and hope in the future. By trusting in God to guide us on our journey, we can celebrate the liberation of forgiveness and start living a life that is truly free.

In the referenced scripture, Micah 7:19–20, the prophet Micah beautifully encapsulates the boundless compassion and steadfast love of God. This scripture reinforces the concept of divine forgiveness, as it promises us God's willingness to not only forgive our iniquities but to submerge them into the depths of the sea, signifying a complete erasure of our transgressions. This profound act of divine mercy resonates deeply with the themes discussed in this chapter. The journey of emotional healing and forgiveness that we've embarked upon in this book is mirrored in God's unending grace, affirming that we too can learn to cast aside resentment, to forgive and forget, and to move forward unburdened by past wounds. Engaging in a process of self-compassion and forgiveness akin to divine mercy, we can find ourselves on a path toward profound emotional liberation and spiritual well-being. There are several steps you can take:

Action Steps

1. **ACKNOWLEDGE YOUR FEELINGS:** Start by recognizing and expressing your emotions rather than suppressing them. It may be challenging initially, but it's an important part of the healing process.

2. **EXPLORE YOUR EMOTIONS:** Allow yourself to explore these feelings without fear or judgment. This will help you identify the root of your pain.

3. **FORGIVE:** The next step involves forgiveness. Forgive yourself and those who have hurt you. This may be difficult, but it's crucial for moving ahead with compassion and understanding. Remember, everyone makes mistakes.

4. **PROCESS AND UNDERSTAND:** After forgiveness, take time to reflect on what happened and why it affected you the way it did. Accept responsibility for your own emotional reactions and recognize how past experiences have shaped you.

5. **MAKE POSITIVE CHANGES:** With this understanding, start making positive changes in your life.

6. **CULTIVATE SELF-LOVE AND ACCEPTANCE:** Finally, practice self-love and acceptance. Be kind to

yourself even when you make mistakes, and know that you deserve love, respect, and joy.

7. **NURTURE SUPPORTIVE RELATIONSHIPS:** Spend time building relationships with those who love and support you, practice positive affirmations, and engage in activities that make you feel good.

The first step in healing emotional wounds is to acknowledge how you feel. This may be difficult at first, but it's important to recognize your emotions and learn to express them rather than suppress them. Allowing yourself to explore your feelings without fear or judgment can help you identify the root of your pain and start the process of healing.

The next step is to forgive yourself and those who have hurt you. It may be hard to forgive someone, but it's important to move forward with compassion and understanding. Remember that everyone makes mistakes; the key is to learn from them and grow.

Once you've forgiven yourself and those around you, you can begin to process and understand your emotions. It's important to take the time to reflect on what happened and why it made you feel the way you did. Once you can accept responsibility for your own emotional reactions and recognize that past experiences have shaped how you think, feel, and behave today, you can start making positive changes in your life.

Finally, it's important to cultivate self-love and acceptance. This means being kind to yourself even when you make mistakes and recognizing that you are worthy of love, respect, and joy. Take the time to nurture relationships with people who love and support you, practice positive affirmations, and do things that make you feel good.

By embracing these steps, you can start to heal your emotional wounds and create a life full of joy, peace, and emotional freedom. Don't be afraid to reach out for help if you need it—you are not alone in this journey. Remember that healing is possible, and with patience, resilience, and faith, you will eventually find your way back to yourself. With every step on this spiritual journey, you are becoming stronger and more capable of creating a meaningful life.

I am thankful for this journey that I am on now. I can honestly say that it has not been the easiest thing to do, but each day I make steps toward improving. I choose to forgive because God commanded us to do so. To my offenders, some of whom have passed away and others who are alive, I choose to forgive because we are both locked into this space of offense that seems frozen in time on a perpetual journey without a destination. I choose to forgive not only to free myself from this psychological and emotional bondage but to release you from my mental prison. I choose to forgive to allow God to deal with the unjust and injury just as He promised. I choose to forgive so that true healing and restoration can begin.

I encourage you, the reader, to do the same. Even if it is only one step at a time, take the journey of forgiveness for yourself and those who have caused you pain or hurt in some way. Release your brokenness and allow God to restore what has been taken away. I believe that forgiveness is possible, and it is the only way to begin true healing from the inside out. So today, choose forgiveness first and don't look back—God has promised to never leave your side. You are worth more than you know, and true healing is within your reach. Today, make the choice to forgive and take action on it.

In life, forgiveness is an essential element for personal growth and inner peace. The liberation that comes with the act of forgiving is one of the greatest gifts that we can give ourselves. Forgiveness is not merely about absolving others for their wrongdoings, but it is also about letting go of our own anger, hurt, and resentment toward them. It is a process that requires courage, introspection, and self-awareness. By forgiving ourselves and others, we cleanse our hearts of negative emotions and free ourselves from the emotional baggage that holds us back. So let us celebrate the liberation of forgiveness in our lives and embrace the peace and love that it brings. The journey toward forgiveness might be challenging, but it is undoubtedly worthwhile. Forgiveness is the key to a fulfilled and happy life.

Take courage, and step into healing your emotional wounds with patience, resilience, and faith. You can create a life full of joy, peace, and emotional freedom that you are capable of cultivating with each step taken on this spiritual journey. You will become stronger and embark on a meaningful voyage with each advance in your expedition. Don't be afraid to ask for help if you need it; you are not alone. Healing is attainable if you maintain optimism—embrace these steps toward transformation so that your transformation can become achievable. Elevate your faith in God's power to heal you, but take the necessary steps to walk in full obedience, allowing forgiveness to open and release you from the prison of unforgiveness.

Reflection Questions

1. How has reading about emotional wounds, forgiveness, boundaries, and toxic relationships impacted my understanding of my own emotional experiences?

2. What are some key takeaways that I can apply to my own life to promote emotional healing and growth?

3. How can I continue to prioritize my emotional well-being and commit to the healing process moving forward?

4. How can I practice empathy and compassion for myself and others as we all navigate our emotional journeys?

5. What can I do to support others who may be struggling with emotional wounds or seeking emotional freedom?

ABOUT *the*
AUTHOR
DR. SAMUEL I. BROWN

D r. Samuel I. Brown, born in the vibrant windy city of Chicago, Illinois, is a multifaceted individual whose life journey has been marked by unwavering dedication to education, ministry, and the written word.

Samuel, born to Pastor Phil Brown and Willie D. Brown, was raised in a close-knit family devoted to Christian values alongside his other siblings. His educational journey took him through various esteemed institutions, including Grace Christian College, Concordia University in River Forest, and Grace Theological Seminary. Samuel's pursuit of knowledge culminated in the achievement of a Bachelor of Science in Christian Education, a Master of Science in Psychology, a Master of Science in Divinity, and a Doctor of Theology degree.

One of Samuel's most noteworthy achievements is his status as a published author, a testament to his commitment to sharing wisdom and insights with the world. His writing talents are matched only by his roles as an educator, administrator, and mentor. With over 17 years of experience, Samuel has worn many educational hats, from being a teacher and dean of students to serving as a principal and advisor, all while leaving an indelible mark on the lives of his students.

Beyond the realm of education, Samuel has dedicated himself to a life of ministry, having been ordained as an Elder, serving as a pastor, administrator, and gifted musician. He has been invited to speak at conferences, revivals, and services in churches across the nation, sharing his profound knowledge and inspiring messages.

Known for his sincerity, tireless work ethic, trustworthiness, loyalty, and compassion, Samuel also has a remarkable sense of humor, embracing laughter as a source of joy. His favorite hobbies include reading, composing music, playing the piano, boxing, and exploring new horizons through travel. As an avid student of the Bible and books on leadership, boxing, education, and more, Samuel's quest for knowledge knows no bounds.

Currently, Samuel is hard at work on his upcoming books, "Bloom Where You're Planted: Discovering Purpose in Every Season of Life" and "Reclaiming Your True Identity." He is also in the process of developing innovative online courses to guide individuals on their journey towards purpose.

Samuel's abiding passion revolves around helping others discover their spiritual purpose and identity in Christ, extending a compassionate hand to those in need, and sharing his knowledge through teaching and coaching. He is dedicated to excellence in administration and constantly strives to be an effective leader and communicator.

With an unwavering commitment to making a meaningful difference in the lives of those around him, Samuel I. Brown is a beacon of inspiration, education, and spiritual guidance, making a meaningful mark wherever his path may lead.

BIBLIOGRAPHY

Amiri, Fateme, Mahboubeh Muslimifar, Esmaeil Showani, and Ali Panahi. "Effectiveness of Forgiveness Therapy in the Treatment of Symptoms of Depression, Anxiety, and Anger among Female Students with Love Trauma Syndrome." *Journal of Advanced Pharmacy Education and Research* 10 (Jan–Mar 2020): 99.

Bash, Anthony. "Forgiveness and Christian Ethics." Philosophical Papers. Accessed October 8, 2015. https://philpapers.org/rec/BASFAC.

Enright, Robert D., and Joanna North. 1998. *Exploring Forgiveness*. Univ of Wisconsin Press.

Enright, Robert D., and Richard P. Fitzgibbons. "The Enright Process Model of Psychological Forgiveness." In *Helping Clients Forgive: An Empirical Guide for Resolving Anger and Restoring Hope*, 65–88. American Psychological Association, 2000. https://truthandlove.com/wp-content/uploads/2017/06/Enright_Process_Forgiveness_1.pdf.

Evans, C. Stephen. "Accountability and the Fear of the Lord." *Studies in Christian Ethics* 34, no. 3 (2021): 316–323.

Fine, Gail. *On Ideas: Aristotle's Criticism of Plato's Theory of Forms.* Kindle. Vol. 104. New York, United States of America: Oxford University Press, 1995. https://doi.org/10.2307/2186014.

Fiske, Susan T., Daniel T. Gilbert, and Gardner Lindzey. 2010. *Handbook of Social Psychology, Volume 2.* John Wiley & Sons.

Gonzales, Michael. "The Role of Emotions in Spiritual Formation." *Journal of Spiritual Formation and Soul Care* 5, no. 2, (2012): 145–158.

Griswold, Charles L. *Forgiveness: A Philosophical Exploration.* New York, United States of America: Cambridge University Press, 2007.

Hickman, Carolyn. *Forgiving When You Can't Forget: Releasing Fear and Trauma from Your Past So You Can Have Freedom in Your Future,* 2021.

Jampolsky, Gerald G. *Forgiveness: The Greatest Healer of All.* New York: Bantam Books, 1999.

Karen, Robert, PhD. *The Forgiving Self: The Road from Resentment to Connection.* New York, United States of America: Anchor Books, 2011.

Lewis, David. "Causation." *The Journal of Philosophy* 70, no. 17 (October 11, 1973): 556. https://doi.org/10.2307/2025310.

Luskin, Frederic. *Forgive for Good: A Proven Prescription for Health and Happiness*. Harper Collins, 2010.

McCullough, Michael. 2008. *Beyond Revenge: The Evolution of the Forgiveness Instinct*. San Francisco, CA, United States of America: John Wiley & Sons.

Merriam-Webster.com Dictionary, s.v. "forgiveness," accessed October 5, 2015, https://www.*Merriam-Webster*.com/dictionary/forgiveness.

Merriam-Webster.com Dictionary, s.v. "unforgiveness," accessed October 7, 2015, https://www.*Merriam-Webster*.com/dictionary/unforgiveness.

Mickley, J. R., and K. Cowles. "Ameliorating the Tension: Use of Forgiveness for Healing." *Oncology Nursing Forum* 28, no. 1 (January 2001): 31–37.

Reed, Gloria J. "Forgiveness as a Path to Healing and Reconciliation." *Journal of Psychology and Christianity*, 33, no. 1 (2014): 59-67.

Smedes, Lewis B. *Forgive and Forget: Healing the Hurts We Don't Deserve*. San Francisco: HarperOne, 2007.

Smedes, Lewis B. *The Art of Forgiving: When You Need to Forgive and Don't Know How*. New York: Ballantine Books, 1996.

Strelan, Peter, and Jan-Willem van Prooijen. "Retribution and Forgiveness: The Healing Effects of Punishing for Just Deserts." *European Journal of Social Psychology* 43, no. 6 (2013): 544–553.

Toussaint, Loren L., E. L. J. Worthington, and David R. Williams. *Forgiveness and health*. Springer Netherlands, 2015.